Winning Strategies
for
Developing Grant Proposals

Government Information Services
an affiliate of Thompson Publishing Group®
1725 K St. N.W., Suite 700
Washington, DC 20006
(202) 872-4000 (Editorial Offices)
(800) 876-0226 (Customer Service)

Winning Strategies
for
Developing Grant Proposals

Editors: Lisa Hayes, Don Hoffman, Denise Lamoreaux
Production Manager: Connie Barclay
Graphic Artist: Todd Bair
Editorial Intern: Emily Worden

Price: $59. Discounts available for quantity purchases. Copies of this book can be obtained from:

Government Information Services
Subscription Service Center
8130 Anderson Rd., Ste. 300
Tampa, FL 33634–2358
(800) 876–0226

Printed in the United States of America. ISBN 0–9670470–4–8

Table of Contents

1 Introduction

As the competition for federal and private grant dollars grows ever more intense, it becomes increasingly important for the grantseeker to present potential funders with a persuasive, thorough and concise grant proposal.

Whether your organization is a local government agency, a community–based nonprofit service group, a private charity or another type of grantseeking entity, knowing how to find – and win – public and private grants can be essential to creating and maintaining projects and services. The federal government and private funders offer billions of dollars in support each year for projects ranging from school improvement and environmental restoration to public safety and services for the elderly. But there is a lot of competition for these grant dollars, and grantseekers must make sure their proposals stand out among the thousands of funding proposals submitted each year.

Winning Strategies for Developing Grant Proposals is intended to help grantseekers obtain a share of grant funding for their organization and programs.

Grantseeking is a challenging and sometimes daunting task. A formal request for funding must present a great deal of information about the organization, the proposed project and the resources that exist in the community to address a specific need. It is this information that a grantmaker will use to determine whether a particular project is appropriate and deserving of support.

The grantseeking process is more than merely presenting a request for funding to a federal agency or a private foundation. It requires extensive research to find a funder that is compatible with your organization's goals and requirements, an assessment of the current needs and services available in the community; and, development of a comprehensive project. Once all of these tasks are accomplished, it is then time to make a formal request for funding.

Winning Strategies for Developing Grant Proposals is intended to take you through each step of the grantseeking process, offering advice and information that can make your grantseeking efforts more efficient and successful. You will find information on how to begin researching potential funding sources, whether they be federal or private. We have also included a list of useful research resources, descriptions of the different types of funders and suggestions for establishing and maintaining your own resource files.

In addition, you will find a discussion regarding the basics of writing a solid proposal. We have included tips from grant proposal reviewers on what the application should contain, advice on how to write the proposal, and a checklist of do's and don'ts. Many grantmakers cite as the leading reason grant proposals fail to get funded is the application's failure to be clear and concise.

Winning Strategies for Developing Grant Proposals also looks at the types of grant programs that are available from the federal government and private givers. In the discussion of private sector sources is an explanation of the various types of foundations that award grant funds, as well as tips on how to select and approach a private sector giver that is appropriate for your organization or project. You will also find a copy of a proposal that was awarded a grant from Newman's Own – actor Paul Newman's charitable foundation.

In the discussion of federal grants you will find an explanation of the various types of grants that are available from the federal government, tips on how and where to find information on available funding and some general grantseeking tips. You will also find a copy of a recent winning federal grant proposal.

To help make your grantseeking job easier, you will find reprints of some of the federal government's standard application forms and an example of a common grant application packet used to apply for private grants.

Throughout the booklet, we have included helpful checklists designed to provide a quick snapshot of the most important elements of a good proposal. Incorporated into all of the discussions is advice from a range of private foundation and corporate grantmaking officials, federal program administrators and grantseeking consultants.

Winning Strategies for Developing Grant Proposals focuses on competitive, or discretionary, federal grant programs, as well as private grantmaking. It does not discuss the grantseeking process for the formula and entitlement grants offered by the federal government or the competitions within states for state and local government funding. You will find as you read this publication, however, that most of the suggestions and advice offered will apply to all of your organization's grantseeking efforts, regardless of the funding source or the application process.

Reader Feedback

We encourage readers to contact us with comments, questions and suggestions about this material. Address remarks to Editor, *Winning Strategies for Developing Grant Proposals*, Government Information Services, 1725 K St. N.W., 7th Floor, Washington, DC 20006; (202) 872–4000; e-mail: **strategies@thompson.com**.

2 Beginning the Grantseeking Process

Before you begin actively pursuing any private or public sector funding, there are several key questions and issues you must address. Not only will you need basic information about your organization, you will have to think honestly about your organization and its mission and ask yourself "Why does my organization need grant funding?" Once you have answered that question, ask yourself "Which funder is most appropriate for my organization's needs?" Successful proposal writers, foundation officials, government administrators and technical assistance experts all agree that there is one key element in the search for funding: do your homework.

Start With a Clearly Defined Goal

To be a successful grantseeker, you must present the potential funding source with a clear picture of why your proposed program is necessary, why your organization is the most suitable to run the program, what are the goals you are trying to reach, how you plan to achieve those goals and how you will measure your success.

Your organization must know exactly what it wants to accomplish and the steps it will take to get there. Never apply for a federal or private sector grant simply because there is money available. Grantseekers must show that they need *funding*. A community need is not the same as a need for funding. In other words, you must show the potential funder that there is a need for *your* program and that your program needs financial support.

You should ask yourself questions such as:

➤ Are there other organizations in the community working to address similar needs?

➤ Why is the community need or the proposed project a priority for our organization?

➤ How would additional funding fill in gaps in current programs and services?

Whether your concern is economic development, substance abuse prevention, adult literacy or housing, taking the time to identify your specific goals and plans will help lead you to an appropriate funding source and will help form the basis of a strong grant proposal.

Weigh the Benefits, "Costs" of Administering Grant Dollars

Never assume that all grant dollars will help your organization. In most cases, federal and private grants may come with "strings" attached. For example, tied to federal grants are numerous rules for such things as accounting, recordkeeping and matching. Complying with these rules takes time and effort to which your organization may or may not want to devote resources. Still, getting your program funded through a federal grant may outweigh the costs of complying with administrative rules. Thus, in determining whether the funding you are seeking is worthwhile, several key questions need to be addressed:

➤ What are the benefits of participating in this program?

➤ Are there any potential drawbacks to participating?

➤ What happens to the project when the funding ends?

➤ How many people and/or departments will be involved in the program and in the application process?

➤ Where does this program and this grant rank in the overall priorities of our organization?

➤ Does the grant and the grantmaker fit within our organization's goals and missions?

This last question is especially important for social service organizations. For instance, a nonprofit dedicated to substance abuse prevention among young people may want to carefully consider whether to seek support from an alcohol manufacturer, even if the funding would be used for a youth alcohol prevention project.

A second general issue that must be realistically addressed is whether your organization is an appropriate grantseeker and whether the request for funding is within the funder's areas of interest, range of awards and type of support.

If your organization is politically or religiously oriented, make sure the proposed project is not. Many funders will not support church groups, fraternal organizations, athletic clubs, political organizations or for-profit groups unless the proposed project is a charitable and "neutral" activity that will benefit the community or a specific group within the community. Further, newly formed organizations that have no track record of serving community needs may have a tough time finding support. If your organization falls into one of these categories, consider working in collaboration with established, nonprofit community groups to develop and implement your project.

In addition, keep in mind that most funders – whether public or private – do not provide grants for general operating expenses, construction or building renovation projects, campaign funds or emergency expenses. Grantmakers usually want to fund specific projects that show signs of creativity and innovation, that can demonstrate measurable goals and that will provide a positive public image for the funder.

Once you have defined your organization's goals and objectives, and are ready to begin the grantseeking process, you will need to decide who will actually write the grant proposal. You may want to consider hiring a grants coordinator – someone whose job responsibility is writing proposals.

The Grants Coordinator

A grants coordinator can help you avoid many of the common mistakes made by novice grantseekers and will have the expertise to guide you to an appropriate source of funding for your organization or project. Such an individual can also help coordinate all of your organization's grantseeking efforts, keep you up to date on a range of federal and private funding opportunities, track current grantmaking trends and serve as a contact point with community leaders, local officials and grant program administrators.

If you decide to use a grants coordinator, you will then have to determine whether hiring a consultant or using in-house staff for grantseeking activities best meets your organization's strategic goals. In making this determination, you will need to assess your budgetary capacity to hire additional staff or contract with a consultant. If your organization's long-term goals include programs that require either federal or private support, it may be wise to delegate grantseeking responsibility to a staff member (either full-time or part-time).

Regardless of whether you choose to use a grants coordinator for your funding search, most experienced grantseekers agree that you should establish a grant proposal library.

What is a Grant Proposal Library?

Put simply, a grant proposal library is a collection of information and resources that your organization has used over the years in its grantseeking efforts. Within this collection you should have copies of all of your proposals – whether they were successful or not – along with any feedback you may have received from funding sources. (*See* The Grant Proposal Library – A Vital Resource, *for ideas on what to include in your collection.*)

Successful grantseekers agree that creating and continuously updating a grant proposal library will dramatically improve your chances of writing a winning proposal. Through this library, you will have easy access not only to what worked in your grantseeking efforts, but also to specific examples of the things that did not work.

In addition, by maintaining a grant proposal library, you will be able to quickly retrieve standard – or "boilerplate" – materials that are required by nearly all federal and foundation grantmakers, such as a listing of your board of directors, staff resumes and annual reports.

Creating a Grant Proposal Library

A word of caution on using boilerplate material. *Never* submit a grant proposal or even a letter of inquiry that you have merely copied from a previous grant proposal. Similarly, do not mass produce generic cover letters or proposal summaries. Every piece of correspondence with a potential grantmaker must be written for the specific funder and project. Boilerplate material should only be used as a framework and for statistical or routine information (such as lists of board members and staff resumes.)

You may find it difficult to obtain some of the information that comprises a grant proposal library, such as examples of other organizations' proposals. Many

The Grant Proposal Library – A Vital Resource

In setting up a grant proposal library, or even just a set of proposal files, you will want to include:

➤ All of your past proposals (winners and losers, too).

➤ Detailed resumes of the entire staff.

➤ Resumes of grants consultants, part-time workers and potential employees.

➤ Proposals prepared by other organizations with similar missions.

➤ All current federal grants management and procurement regulations.

➤ Any books, reports, memoranda and similar documents regarding the submission of proposals, contracts and bids.

➤ Detailed descriptions of all current and past projects and contracts on which your organization makes regular reports.

➤ Any available and pertinent personnel directories from federal agencies and private funders.

➤ Information about your own organization, including a mission statement, organizational chart and history.

➤ Annual reports, program guidelines and application procedures of foundations and corporate funders.

private-sector grantmakers are happy to send out copies of their annual reports, for example, but will not provide you with copies of proposals that have been submitted to them.

One reason for grantmakers' reluctance to hand out proposals is the desire to protect the privacy of applicants. One possible solution is to contact organizations that have recently received support from the grantmaker and ask them for copies of their proposals. In many instances, organizations that have applied for funding from a particular foundation or corporate giver are willing to share their experiences with you.

If you are searching for information on federal grant programs, you may be forced to file a Freedom of Information Act (FOIA) request. Federal programs – especially those that are currently considered "priorities" – may include examples of winning grant proposals in their application materials or in the background information they provide about the program. However, if you find that a particular agency does not provide all of the information you need, filing a FOIA may be an option.

Freedom of Information Act

Under the Freedom of Information Act, virtually every record of a federal agency must be made available to the public upon written request. Agencies may deny FOIA requests in certain instances, such as disclosures that pertain to law enforcement records or personal information. By law, the agency must process a FOIA request within 20 business days. This does not mean the agency must provide the requested information within that time, merely that it should process the request. In practice, some agencies have a backlog of requests and may take longer to respond.

You should also keep in mind that there may be fees associated with a FOIA request. The agency has the authority to charge you "reasonable standard" fees for costs such as searches, reproduction of materials and delivery.

For that reason, when filing a FOIA request, you should be as specific as possible. For example, filing a FOIA request for information on grant recipients under the Department of Housing and Urban Development's (HUD) Youthbuild program could result in thousands of pages of information and a sizable bill for "reasonable standard" fees.

To avoid this, tailor your request, for example, by asking for information on grant recipients in a particular geographic area. This will result in far fewer documents, cost considerably less, and provide you with plenty of information.

Another way to control the costs of a FOIA request is to clearly state on your request that you would like to be notified if the "reasonable standard" fees are expected to exceed a certain amount, for example, $25. By doing this, the agency is required to notify you of the costs in advance and you can more closely tailor your request so that it does not exceed your budget.

There is no standard FOIA form or required application.

A FOIA request must be made in writing to a federal agency. In most instances, the request can also be transmitted by fax. Some agencies, although not all, are also able to process FOIA requests received over the World Wide Web, but you should check with the agency's FOIA officer first.

Your request should include a detailed explanation of the material you are seeking (include names, dates, grant program, etc.). In addition, your request should include your postal address, the name of the person who will be responsible for paying any fees that may be charged and a phone number where you can be reached to clarify any questions the FOIA officer may have.

Requests should be mailed to the FOIA Officer at the agency from which you are requesting information and should state clearly on the envelope "Freedom of Information Act Request."

Of course, if you have any questions about the FOIA process, or are not sure how to write the request, contact the FOIA officer at the agency to which you will be submitting the request.

Those interested in filing a FOIA with any agency should contact the U.S. Department of Justice's Office of Information and Privacy, (202) 514-3642, for guidance or to receive a list of agency FOIA officers. This information is also available online at **http://www.usdoj.gov/foia**.

Putting together a comprehensive grant proposal library may involve a great deal of work, but the results can save you a significant amount of time and frustration in the future.

3 Basics of Good Proposal Writing

Many requests for funding – whether they are submitted to the federal government or to a private funder – are rejected not because the proposed project is unworthy, but because the applicant failed to follow the basic rules for writing a good grant proposal. The application you submit to a potential funder is your one opportunity to present a complete description of your project, its impact on the community, the qualifications of your organization and the need for your project. Your application or request for funding is a reflection not only of your proposed project but also your organization as a whole.

A poorly planned project or one that does not fit a grantmaker's requirements will not be funded, regardless of how well you present your case to a grantmaker. In contrast, however, the most innovative, needy and well-managed project can be rejected simply because the grant writer fails to follow certain basic rules. As one foundation official noted, "you only get one shot" to present your case in the grant proposal. Make certain that your proposal is the most accurate, well-written and thorough document you can offer.

You need to follow a step-by-step process in your grantwriting efforts. It takes time and persistence to write a good proposal.

The first step in writing a good grant proposal is to gather all of the information you will need at one location. This means you will have to collect background information on your organization, including data such as financial reports, proof of public or private nonprofit status, a list of your board of directors and resumes of key project staff.

Larger nonprofit organizations and public agencies should have most of this information on file, but if you work for a small nonprofit, you may have to ask other individuals to help you gather this information. Members of your board of directors and program staff within your organization, for example, can be valuable contacts during the proposal writing process. In addition, maintaining a grants proposal library, or a collection of basic information needed for all of your grantseeking efforts, is a good way to handle this fact-finding task. (*See Chapter 2 for more information on establishing a grants proposal library.*)

Rule Number One: Follow Instructions

The first rule of good grantwriting is: *follow the grantmaker's guidelines.* This may sound like obvious advice, but public and private program administrators say they frequently receive proposals and applications from organizations that are not eligible or from groups requesting funds for projects that fall outside their giving guidelines. Still other proposals simply do not follow all of the instructions provided by the grantmaker.

"It's a real shame when a good project doesn't get funded simply because they didn't follow directions," said one foundation official. "It's hard to tell if grantseekers just don't understand how important our guidelines are or if they just don't take the time to read them or if they think their project is so important that they don't have to follow the rules. We develop giving guidelines for a reason," he said.

Funders prefer various formats for the full proposal. These requirements usually will be specified in the notice inviting applications or in the grantmaker's giving guidelines. The funder will tell you what forms and certifications must be included, provide a specific list of the questions that should be addressed in your proposal, tell you how many copies to submit and tell you when and where to submit your proposal. Pay careful attention to these requirements.

You should also determine if the funder requires any specific format for a proposal. Some grantmakers will indicate whether proposals must be single- or double-spaced, the size and style of the font to be used, and the page limitation.

Following these guidelines can be extremely important. As mentioned above, funders establish guidelines for a reason. One recent request for proposals from an environmental group indicated that applicants should use a small type size and use both sides of the sheet of paper. Applicants who chose to ignore this format had no chance of winning funding. The reason for these requirements was the grantmaker's desire to conserve paper, an obvious goal of an environmental group.

When you answer the grantmaker's questions in the order asked and follow the format provided, you make the donor's job much easier. You also show respect for the funder, a willingness to meet any requirements that may be part of the grantseeking and award process and that you can follow directions.

Standard Elements of a Proposal

If the funder does not give you specific instructions on what to include in your proposal, at a minimum, you should include the following information.

➤ **Cover letter.** Identify yourself and your organization, and indicate the reason for the application, i.e., you are requesting funding to support your project.

➤ **Introduction.** Briefly provide a short and clear statement of what is to be accomplished through your project, the need for your project and the link between your project and the funder's areas of interest. As the first page of your proposal, the introduction is a key to whether your search for funding will be successful. Here you must provide the reader with a quick overview of your project and make the reviewer want to continue reading your proposal. Consider this your "sales pitch." In one page, you must convince the reader that your project deserves to be funded by presenting the problem, your proposed solution, how much money you are requesting and how your organization is qualified to handle the project.

➤ **Background.** Tell the potential funder why the project is needed. This section of the proposal, which is sometimes called the problem statement, is the area where you should clearly define the specific problem to be addressed. Then go on to identify the individuals (or class of individuals) who will benefit from your project, discuss the degree to which the problem is being addressed (or not addressed) by other groups in the community and explain why your organization is best equipped to implement the proposed project.

To write the background section of your application, you will need to conduct a needs assessment in the community. One federal official noted that conducting a thorough needs assessment – which specifically identifies the problem, why it exists, what needs to be done, the services that are currently available to address the problem and who would benefit from your project – is essential in developing an effective project.

Once you have a needs assessment, and therefore, understand the problem and what needs to be done, said the federal official,

What a Proposal Should Include

✓ Cover letter
✓ Introduction
✓ Background
✓ Organizational history
✓ Objectives
✓ Plan of operation
✓ Evaluation
✓ Budget

actually writing a grant proposal should be the easy part. There are several ways to gather information for a needs assessment, including conducting surveys of potential program participants, sponsoring discussion meetings with community services agencies and researching statistical databases.

Grantwriters advise that you avoid the use of "circular reasoning" in which you assert that the problem is the fact that your project does not exist. For instance, if you are seeking funding to support an after-school program aimed at keeping at-risk youth away from crime and violence, do not say that the problem is a lack of after-school services and that the solution is to fund your project.

Instead, tell the potential funder that youth crime rates during non-school hours are increasing and indicate that there is a shortage of after-school centers where children can be in a safe, supervised environment. Then show how your proposed project would address this issue by offering students a positive alternative to crime, violence and drugs. Cite examples of how after-school projects in other communities have reduced juvenile crime rates or tell how a small-scale demonstration project has worked in your own community, if one has been undertaken.

➤ **Organizational history.** In a brief statement, describe your organization, its background, its mission statement and, if appropriate, a statement regarding your organization's status as a public or private nonprofit entity.

➤ **Objectives.** This section of your proposal should explain what you plan to achieve through your project. Describe specific goals and what impact you believe the proposed project will have in the community.

➤ **Plan of operation.** The plan of operation, or project description, should detail the specific steps your organization will take in developing and implementing the project. Be sure to include a timeline under which you expect to accomplish each of the steps you describe in the plan. This is also a good place to describe the skills and qualifications of key staff members who will be working on the project and to describe how you will work with other organizations in the community to meet your project's goals.

It may be difficult to describe the need for your project and the plans that your organization has for addressing the issue without being critical of other organizations in your community that are working toward the same goals. But you should avoid such tactics at all costs.

Being critical of other public and nonprofit agencies is something that most grant-makers disapprove of. In fact, working in partnership with other agencies, rather than highlighting their shortcomings, can actually be a benefit. Funders are very interested in collaboration. If you are not part of a partnership or collaborative project, your proposal may be rejected because the funders question why you have not considered working with other nonprofits in your community.

Many grants consultants and program officials say one of the best things you can do to strengthen your proposal is to show that you are working in collaboration with other agencies and organizations in the community. Collaboration, coalition, partnership – whatever you call it – the concept of public and private agencies working together is becoming more and more popular with private, as well as federal, funders.

One state official who was successful in raising funds for a collaborative social services improvement project said approaching a project as a collaborative effort can help you focus on what you want to achieve. As you form the partnership, you will be forced to specifically define your project's goals and outcome measures and to delineate the steps that you will take.

But be prepared. There can be some challenges in establishing partnerships. Agencies may enter into "turf battles" over project activities. Each participating partner must be assigned specific project activities and responsibilities. There can also be a lot of paperwork and planning time involved in recruiting and engaging multiple partners.

Such concerns can be addressed by making sure that all participating agencies completely understand the goals and methodologies of the project and that they know what their responsibilities will be.

You can eliminate confusion by entering into a memorandum of understanding (MOU) with all of your project's partners. This MOU will spell out the specific responsibilities of each partner, such as time involvement, staff participation and financial obligations. You can also solicit letters of support from your partners. In these letters, the partner organizations should spell out their commitment to the project as well as provide an outline of their level of participation. Once the MOU or letter of support is signed by all parties, it can serve as evidence of a formal collaboration.

When you form a collaboration or partnership, you can save yourself time and repetitive efforts by addressing any issues the funder may have about your partners up front. For example, in the appendices of your proposal, include letters of support and memorandums of understanding specifying the roles and responsibilities of each agency. Also include proof of nonprofit status for each partner, if appropriate and requested, as well as brief descriptions of each partner.

It is important that members of a collaboration do not appear to be competing for funds. In your narrative, you must show the potential funder that the partners will be working together to achieve the project's goals. According to one private foundation official, most funders are not interested in how the grant funds will be distributed among the partners. Foundation officials are looking for results.

It may seem like a lot of work to develop a detailed plan of operation, but according to many program administrators, one of the main reasons proposals fail to win grants is that they contain insufficient information about how the project will be carried out. Generally, the more detail you can provide in your proposal, the better. These details show that you have thoroughly thought out the proposed project and will give grant reviewers a firm idea of what you are trying to accomplish.

➤ **Evaluation plan.** Many grants consultants say grantseekers too often gloss over this section of their proposal. In fact, it is one of the most important elements of the proposal. A good evaluation plan will spell out the specific steps you will take to critique the program to measure its success – or failure. All funders want to know that their resources are being used effectively. You must specifically describe how you plan to judge the effectiveness of your project and, if necessary, make changes based on the assessment. Private funders are placing an increased emphasis on the evaluation component of projects as they seek ways to gain the maximum impact from their philanthropic efforts. Similarly, the federal government is striving to hold all of its program offices and grantees accountable for the use of public tax dollars.

When developing the evaluation plan, list the specific measures that you will use to judge the effectiveness of your project. Grants experts recommend that you use between three and 10 specific measures for evaluation. If, for example, the goal of your proposed project is to reduce the level of crimes committed by youth during nonschool hours, appropriate measures could include the number of juvenile arrests, truancy rates and the number of students participating in extracurricular activities.

Many funding experts also recommend that you develop an ongoing evaluation plan, rather than one that merely measures the end result of the project. This will allow you to make changes to the project, if needed, rather than waiting until the project is completed to find out whether it was effective. If you measure the progress you are making at various stages of the project, you can make adjustments that will allow you to achieve the ultimate goal, rather than wasting time on an ineffective activity. But, remember to include in any ongoing evaluation plan a mechanism through which the funder is kept aware of any changes you make to the originally funded project.

You may also want to consider the possibility of offering your project as a model for other agencies and communities. Doing so may broaden your appeal to grantmakers because most funders are looking to support innovative projects and to maximize the reach of their grant dollars. Beware, however, that being a model project may require an additional investment of time and resources. You may be required to develop a plan for replicating your project in other communities and you will probably be asked to participate in a large-scale evaluation. Your organization may be asked to offer technical assistance and training to other agencies that want to adopt your project.

➤ **Budget.** Be as detailed as possible when developing your budget. And do not forget to ask for a specific amount of support. You might be surprised to learn that many grantseekers actually forget to include a specific funding request in their proposals. Ask the funder for a specific contribution and give an itemized description of how the funding will be used.

Be sure to include information about your organization's overall budget and your other sources of funding. You will also want to include a listing of any in-kind contributions of volunteer time or donated materials that will be used to support the project. And, if the potential funder requires a match, do not forget to clearly indicate any funds (or in-kind services) that your organization is providing as that match. Your budget should also include your plans for continuing the project after the grant period ends, if appropriate. Funders want to know the project will not be abandoned once their contribution has ended.

One final note: make certain that the dollar amounts cited in your budget add up. Nothing can destroy credibility like inaccurate budget information.

Tips for Writing a Successful Proposal

✓ Choose a program title that concisely and accurately reflects the goals of your project.

✓ Follow directions. Read the grantmaker's guidelines carefully so that you understand what information is required. Follow any guidelines for format.

✓ Pay attention to deadlines. Remember that application deadlines are firm. In some instances, the grantmaker will ask that you *mail* your proposal by a specified date and will accept proof of mailing – such as a receipt from the U.S. Post Office – as evidence that you met the deadline. In other instances, the funder may require that your proposal arrive by the deadline date. Allow sufficient time for your application to be delivered.

✓ Read the proposal in its entirety before submitting it, especially if different people are contributing portions of the written proposal. If possible, ask someone who did not work on the proposal to proofread it for errors and clarity.

✓ Keep the proposal's language simple and clear.

✓ Include tables, charts and diagrams when appropriate. However, use them only when they support your proposal. Charts and tables should not be used as fluff material.

✓ Include large volumes of data as appendices. Inserting a vast amount of statistical information in the text of a narrative slows down the reader and makes your proposal seem complicated.

✓ Be sure to explain all abbreviations and terms that someone outside your organization may not understand.

✓ Make sure the final copy is neat, free of typographical errors and presented in a professional style.

Do Not Go Overboard

As you write your grant proposal, keep in mind that federal and private program officials are often called on to review hundreds of proposals. Many grantmakers say they simply do not have the time or personnel to read exhaustive manuscripts. Even if the potential funder has not established a page limit for the grant application, try to keep your proposal as concise as possible.

While you must address all of the elements listed above in a thorough manner, try not to be too wordy. Put yourself in the reviewers' shoes, advises one foundation official. "I don't think most foundations want to receive five-inch thick proposals," she said. "We really only have time to stick to the basics."

Writing the Narrative

The narrative describing your proposed project is the cornerstone of the grant proposal. Many grantseekers – both experienced and novice – find that writing the narrative section of an application can be the most difficult part of developing a proposal. Providing information such as budget information and background about key project staff is fairly straightforward. But writing a narrative description of your proposed project in a way that is effective, concise and persuasive can be a daunting task.

As one official noted, the best way to approach the narrative is to just begin writing. Get all of your thoughts down on paper, without concern for format and style. That will come later as you refine your proposal.

Do not be intimidated by the writing process. Grant officials say they are not looking for "glitzy" writing in the narrative. What they want is clear writing that is backed by facts. Proposals that are easy to understand have a better chance of receiving funding than those that require the grant reader to slog through confusing, inaccurate or overly wordy materials.

You can strengthen the narrative section of your proposal by following some basic guidelines, which should apply to any writing that you do.

➢ **Get to the point.** Do not save the best for last. Remember that proposal reviewers are looking at many requests for funding and they need to know immediately the problem your project would address, your plan of operation and what type of assistance you need.

➢ **Be honest.** Some grantseekers think they can increase their chances of winning funding if they exaggerate the success of past projects or the organization's achievements. In fact, one grant official said that the applicant who makes all of its work sound like success stories is actually hurting its own credibility.

Nothing is ever 100 percent successful or effective, and admitting that your organization has had less than perfect experiences can also show what you have learned from the past. Sometimes knowing what does not work is as important as knowing what does work, one official said.

➢ **Use simple sentences, short paragraphs and an active, rather than a passive, tense.** In writing your narrative, remember that the reviewer will be reading dozens, and possibly hundreds, of proposals. Do not weigh the reviewer down with long, run-on sentences. Use short and crisp sentences. Make the point and move on.

Also, be sure to keep your paragraphs short. Nothing can distract a reviewer's attention quicker than looking at a sheet of paper that is covered in black ink. Leave some white space to allow the reviewer's eyes a break.

And, most important, use an active, rather than passive tense. Write about what your organization *will* do with the funding. Be positive and optimistic. Let your writing style get the reviewer excited about your proposal.

Finally, think about the reviewer when you write. Consider that the individual reviewing your proposal may not be an expert in your field. If you have to explain complex concepts, do so as clearly and briefly as possible. Avoid the use of jargon and phrases that the reviewer may not know.

By presenting information in a way that the reviewer can understand, you demonstrate that you, too, understand the issues and that your organization is capable of carrying out the proposed project. If the reviewers cannot understand the intent of the proposed project, it is hard for them to judge the merits of the proposed project.

➤ **Be specific.** Do not use vague, imprecise terms or make generalizations. Support all of your claims with facts. Reviewers want facts on which to base their judgment, not rhetoric. Hard data lend credibility to your proposal and will show how your community is being impacted by the problem being addressed. Whenever possible, use both national and local statistics that show how your community is being impacted.

For example, if you are seeking support for a project aimed at reducing youth crime by offering after-school activities, you might want to include a statement similar to the following.

Nationwide, in 1997, juveniles accounted for 19 percent of all arrests and 17 percent of arrests for violent crimes. Overall, an estimated 2.8 million children in the United States were arrested in 1997. The problem in Smith Town is even worse. According to the most recent statistics, 22 percent of the crimes in our county are committed by young people under the age of 18. Further, nearly two-thirds of those crimes are committed between the hours of 3 p.m. and 7 p.m., times when students are not in school.

Be sure that the data you include are accurate and up to date and that they support your project. Adding unnecessary details slows down the reader and may cause confusion.

Another tip for writing a successful narrative: prepare a draft version of the document and have other members of your organization critique it. Ask them to pretend they are a proposal reviewer and to give you constructive criticism on the proposal, identifying any weaknesses in the proposed project or in the writing.

Of course, you must be willing to accept the criticisms and revise your narrative accordingly. For the sake of your proposed project, do not take these criticisms personally – learn from them. It is far better to have a co-worker or peer criticize your work while it can be revised, than to have a funder reject your proposal because you were not willing to make revisions.

Pay Attention to Details

It may sound simple, but using correct grammar, proofreading your proposal for spelling and typographical errors and otherwise following the rules of proper English are essential when you are writing a grant proposal. Do not let your proposal be rejected because it is full of misspelled words. "It certainly doesn't help if you can't even spell our organization's name correctly," commented one grantmaking official.

It can also help to have someone outside your organization read the proposal. By looking at the proposal with a fresh eye, a "neutral party" can look at the overall presentation. They should make certain that the proposal makes sense and that there are no unanswered questions.

Your proposal should be neatly typed and proofread several times. Funders say they continue to receive applications whose sloppy presentation causes reviewers to question the applicant's ability to carry out the project effectively and efficiently. "We do, to some extent, judge a book by its cover," said one official. "Your proposal must be presented in a neat and professional manner."

When Should You Begin Writing the Proposal

The guidelines for any particular program will list upcoming deadlines. In most cases, deadlines fall only once, or sometimes, twice a year. In addition, some grantmakers will ask you to submit a "notice of intent to apply." This notice gives the grantmaker an idea of how many organizations will be applying and allows staff to prepare for the upcoming review. In most cases, you will have to submit a notice of intent several weeks before the formal proposal is due.

In addition, some applicants may be asked to file a brief preliminary proposal to help the grantmaker determine the eligibility of potential applicants or to judge the appropriateness of potential projects.

Assume the deadlines listed by the grantmaker are *firm.* Proposals that fail to meet the deadlines will not be considered. Therefore, it is worth your time to begin preparing your application well in advance of the final deadline. Federal grant competitions normally set deadlines 45 days to 60 days after they are officially announced. However, in some cases, the lead time may be substantially shorter – as little as 30 days.

How far in advance you begin preparing your application depends on the complexity of the application requirements, the scope of your proposed project and the amount of planning and outside cooperation that will be necessary to develop your proposal. Some grantwriters suggest that if possible you begin at least two months in advance. Be aware, however, that you will have to start much earlier than that if you are planning a major undertaking (such as a building renovation) that will require the support and participation of many agencies and individuals.

In addition, funding programs that require you to provide matching resources also require a great deal of development time because you have to demonstrate a plan showing how you will generate additional resources for the project.

Summary of Proposal Writing Do's and Don'ts

Do:

✓ Make sure you are an eligible entity and identify yourself as such in the proposal.

✓ Provide details of the roles and responsibilities of each partner and program staff member. Include any letters of support and memorandum of understanding from partner organizations.

✓ Address in the narrative *all* of the selection criteria specified by the grantmaker.

✓ Write clearly, using subheads and short paragraphs.

✓ Have the proposal read for clarity and typographical errors.

✓ Provide a budget for each year if you are requesting funding for a multi-year project.

✓ Be specific about goals, objectives and evaluation measures.

Don't:

✗ Miss the deadline.

✗ Forget to sign your application.

✗ Exceed the page count for the proposal narrative, if one is specified.

✗ Propose a program that does not meet the funder's specific areas of interest or program objective.

✗ Request more than the funder will give, if such an amount is specified.

✗ Request funds for activities that the funder will not support.

✗ Forget to include all required assurances and supplementary information, such as proof of nonprofit status.

4 Winning Grants From Private Sector Sources

In 1997, foundations and corporations contributed an estimated $21.6 billion to public nonprofit organizations around the country, according to a report from *Giving USA*. Cash contributions, as well as in-kind support such as volunteers and equipment donations, can be a vital part of a nonprofit organization's budget. In the past, many corporations and foundations might have been willing to fund lesser quality, "B-grade" proposals. Now, said one foundation official, with the grantseeking climate becoming more competitive, grantmakers are looking to fund only top quality, "A+" applications.

So, how do you approach a private sector funder when you are trying to win grants for your organization's projects and activities?

The first step is research.

For example, a successful grantseeker must understand that there are several different types of funding entities and that they all have their own goals, sources of income, grantmaking processes and giving patterns. The Internal Revenue Service makes a distinction between public charities and private foundations, but in most cases, they all call themselves "foundations."

> **Private, independent foundations** are often founded by individuals or families. Many of these foundations have been created to address a specific target population or to address a specific topic. For example, the Robert Wood Johnson Foundation, one of the largest grantmakers in the United States, focuses its giving on large-scale projects that will improve health care and the health care system.

> **Community foundations**, on the other hand, are locally established organizations that draw their resources from a variety of donors and contribute funds for a wide array of projects that benefit residents of the community or region. These local grantmakers are a good place to begin your search for private sector funding.

> According to recent statistics, these 547 public charities, as they are called, had assets totaling nearly $21.3 billion in 1997 and awarded more than $1.25 billion in grants. The largest community foundation in the nation is the New York Community Trust, followed by the Greater Kansas City Community Foundation and the San Francisco Foundation.

> For more information on community foundations and their giving activities, contact the Columbus Foundation and Affiliated Trusts, (614) 251-4000, or visit the trusts online at **http://www.columbusfoundation.org/survey_intro.html**.

> **Corporate foundations or corporate giving programs** constitute the third major category of private sector grantmakers. Such entities are typically funded by, but legally separate from, their parent companies. Corporate givers tend to make donations to organizations in their operating communities and usually have a specific giving goal in mind. Corporate givers are more likely to support projects that advance their own business goals, such as developing a well-prepared workforce, improving employee morale and attendance, enhancing their image in the community and creating an economic environment in which their operations can flourish.

Every funder also has its own grant solicitation process, application requirements, giving guidelines and funding limitations. For example, some funders will accept unsolicited requests for funding and donations at any time, while others may only consider applications that are submitted in response to a request for proposals (RFP). The RFP will give specific information about the types of projects to be funded, eligibility, deadlines and application formats.

It may seem like obvious advice, but meeting as many of a funder's program goals, priorities and required project activities as possible can be a key to winning private sector support for your project.

Under one recent RFP, a corporate foundation received more than 600 applications and funded just 54 applicants. Who received funding? Those organizations that met all four of the goals stated in the foundation's RFP. The proposals that addressed only one or two program priorities had no chance of winning support, a foundation official said.

Keep in mind, also, that bigger is not always better.

Grants consultants say there is no correlation between the physical size of a proposal and the project's quality or its chances of winning. Many grants have been awarded on the basis of a two- or three-page project summary supported by a cover letter and background information. In contrast, massive proposals that run, for example, 50 pages or more, can actually turn off a funder. That said, though, it should be noted that one recent successful proposal for a federal housing grant exceeded 1,000 pages.

Always check with the potential funder to determine if there are any page limitations or if they have a preference regarding how large your proposal should be. (See Chapter 3, *Basics of Good Proposal Writing*, for additional tips on how to present your proposal.)

How to Approach Foundations

Here are some tips for determining which foundations are most likely to fund your project.

➤ **Assess any funding limitations or restrictions.** Does the grantmaker limit its activities to a certain geographic region, a certain target audience or a particular type of recipient?

➤ **Select a funder whose "size" is appropriate.** Many large, well-known foundations typically give more funding to high-profile, large-scale projects. It may be a "tough sell" for a small, local grantseeker to successfully present a grant proposal to a large funder, one grants consultant said.

➤ **Make sure your project meets the funder's goals.** No matter how well-thought-out or innovative your program may be, if it does not address the giver's goals, it will not be funded.

➤ **Find out if the funder has an interest in your project before you submit a full proposal.** Most grantmakers encourage you to send in brief letters of inquiry or to make a phone call to a program official before submitting a proposal. Such contact will benefit both you and the funder by eliminating the possibility that you will submit a proposal that has no chance of getting funded. Said one foundation official, if you have a question about the funder's goals and priorities, how your project might fit in, the application guidelines or anything else, just ask. Most foundations want to help you develop a good proposal.

➤ **Develop a relationship with the potential funder.** It may be a cliché, but people give to people, said one foundation official. You should actually view the submission of a formal grant proposal as the "wrap up" of your grantseeking process.

How to Approach Corporations

Although corporations currently account for only a small percentage of private giving in the United States, their cash and in-kind support may be worth investigating, especially if your project is a high-profile endeavor that will benefit the company's bottom line.

In many ways, the process for seeking corporate support is similar to the approach you must take when seeking support from a private or community foundation. You have to check giving limitations, grant size and funding priorities, and you must establish a relationship with the potential funder.

Unlike foundations, however, corporate givers often offer a range of support mechanisms.

One of the most significant and often overlooked aspects of corporate support is non-cash donations. When evaluating your grantseeking options, consider asking for donations of company materials. A local hardware company, for example, might not hand out cash grants but might be willing to donate materials for a public housing rehabilitation project.

Likewise, many companies are now learning the benefits of allowing their employees to volunteer for projects such as installing computers in schools, serving in food kitchens, cleaning up neighborhood parks and counseling at-risk youth.

You should also remember that corporations and businesses are often headed by a single individual or a small group of individuals and that giving programs and the selection of grantees may be based on one individual's personal interests.

One corporate official said giving has become "serious business" and that grantmakers are looking to support organizations that treat it as such.

Some of the major questions corporate officials will ask themselves when they look at your proposal are:

➤ Does the problem to be addressed by the project affect one of our operating communities?

➤ Does the organization use its funds effectively? Grantees must be accountable and must produce results, with both the grant requested and with their current operating funds.

➤ Are there opportunities to leverage our resources? The goal is to maximize every dollar donated by the company so that projects can assist as many individuals as possible. Grantseekers who are willing to work with schools, community groups, local businesses, religious organizations and other institutions are looked upon more favorably. Holding special adult literacy classes at a local school's gymnasium, for example, is a good way to show that your organization can use a wide array of resources to support your project.

➤ How will funding the proposed project add value to our business? Companies – and their grantmaking entities – are looking to improve their bottom line. To do this, companies look for projects that enhance employee skills and leadership abilities, make the community a better place in which to live, increase the potential workforce or consumer base, or otherwise benefit the grantmaking company.

One Winning Proposal

If you follow the advice in this chapter, your chances of writing a winning proposal should be greatly increased. Remember, too, that you must always follow the basics of good grantwriting discussed in Chapter 3.

Always follow the funder's guidelines in preparing your proposal. And, remember that even though different funders prefer different formats and require different information, all prospective donors want clear, concise proposals. Use specific data to demonstrate your need; avoid general statements. Include clear objectives and goals, and specify the steps you will take to reach those goals. If appropriate, include endorsements and supplementary material that will support your request for funding. Be as accurate and specific as possible, being sure to present the funder with all of the information that has been requested. Do not forget to include plans for monitoring and evaluating your project.

To give you an idea of what a winning proposal looks like, on the following pages you will find an actual request for funding that was submitted to Newman's Own, Inc., a grantmaking entity established by actor Paul Newman and funded with proceeds from the sale of his line of specialty food items.

Newman's Own supports projects in the areas of education, social services, health and the environment. The grantmaker is unique in that it is not a nonprofit foundation and does not receive support from corporate investments. It is a giving program of the corporation. In fact, the more money made by the company, the more grants it makes. A foundation official said the company has not established specific guidelines for its grantmaking activities. Instead, Newman himself selects projects for funding based on his personal interests.

Applicants are required to submit their proposals by a specific date and are asked to provide basic information, such as name and address, contact information, any previous support from the company and certain income and expense statistics. Also required is a detailed project budget, a specific funding amount request, a copy of the IRS Letter of Determination indicating nonprofit status and the most recent audited financial statement.

This proposal for funding to renovate facilities at a center serving developmentally disabled individuals was awarded third place in a recent Grantsmanship Center proposal writing contest. Newman's Own has no specific giving guidelines or standard application forms, so there is no formal rating system, so to speak, said a grantmaking official. But what makes this proposal stand out from hundreds of others received by the grantmaker each year is that it is well-organized, easy to understand and it addresses specific questions and needs.

The proposal is well-written and includes very specific information about the need for additional living space and an enclosed swimming pool. There is no unnecessary padding in the proposal. A key factor in the success of this proposal is the fact that the applicant is willing to provide in-kind services to leverage the grantmaker's cash contribution.

Allegany Arc

A resource and career opportunity center
35 years and still growing with our community

Richard S. Witkowski
Executive Director

240 O'Connor Street
Wellsville, NY 14895

Phone: 716-593-5700
Fax: 716-593-4529

August 26, 1998

Mr. Paul Newman — Newman's Own
246 Post Road East
Westport, CT 06880

Dear Mr. Newman,

Please find enclosed a proposal from the Allegany Arc, A Resource and Career Center for the developmentally disabled of Allegany County in western New York. This proposal will benefit 117 developmentally disabled individuals. It involves conversion of an attached, existing garage into living space and enclosure of an existing pool, which would attach to the garage (living space). We are requesting assistance from you in the amount of $12,160. Arc will contribute $13,625 in labor costs. The agency's maintenance staff will complete the renovations. Thus, for every dollar requested from Newman's Own, Arc will match $1.12!

This residence, known as Niles Hill, is home for five developmentally disabled adults. (The other 112 benefiting live in one of Arc's other residences or are enrolled in one of the agency's day programs.) This home is very small and has limited living space. The basement cannot be certified (useable) space per certifying agencies (due to only one exit), nor can the individuals access it due to disabilities and age.

The weather in western New York is so unpredictable and thus, pool use cannot be maximized. There are very few days when it can be used. It is very difficult to schedule using the pool at the local school as the school has priority. All 117 individuals are in need of physical therapy and/or range of motion activities. Water therapy is ideal and most recommended as it is easier and less stressful on the body. This would be most beneficial to individuals dependent on wheelchairs as this pool would be wheelchair accessible; the school pool is not.

Newman's Own can make this project a reality for just $103.93 per person. It will allow year round pool use to all 117 of these individuals and provide them with the opportunity to stay agile and therefore independent longer. This project needs your assistance!

Thank you for the opportunity to apply for funding and for considering our proposal. More importantly, thank you for your support of the developmentally disabled of Allegany County. If I can be of any further assistance, please contact me.

Sincerely,

Margaret L. Winans
Vice President of Giving

*[**Editor's note:** The Allegany Arc included in its proposal financial statements and IRS Form 990. They are not reprinted here.]*

Please attach this form to the front of funding proposal

NAME & ADDRESS OF NON-PROFIT ORGANIZATION
Allegany Arc
240 O'Connor Street
Wellsville, NY 14895
(716) 593-5700

CONTACT PERSON, TITLE & TELEPHONE NUMBER
Margaret L. Winans
Vice President of Giving
(716) 593-5700

NAME OF SPECIAL PROJECT, IF ANY, FOR WHICH FUNDS ARE REQUESTED
Niles Hill

AMOUNT REQUESTED
$12,160
Please note: The Allegany Arc is willing to contribute an in-kind labor contribution
of $13,625.

PREVIOUS SUPPORT
None

MISSION
The Allegany Arc is dedicated to providing opportunities to people with special needs and their families that will assist in improving the quality of their lives. As an advocate, the Arc will provide support and services, ensuring each person the opportunity to learn, achieve, contribute and lead.

PROPOSAL SUMMARY
To renovate the existing attached garage with living space for five developmentally disabled individuals living in the home. Also to enclose the existing pool, which will become attached to the garage. This will benefit 117 individuals in need of physical therapy and range of motion.

Faxed proposals are not accepted.

PLEASE NOTE: Materials submitted, including videos, are nonreturnable.

ORGANIZATIONAL INFORMATION

Agency: Allegany Arc
240 O'Connor Street
Wellsville, NY 14895
(716) 593-5700

Contact: Margaret L. Winans, Vice President of Giving, (716) 593-5700

Area to be served: Allegany County

Previous grants from Salad King, Inc.: None

Percentage of administrative overhead: 8 percent
fund raising: 4 percent

(SEE ATTACHED SHEET)

Percentage of income applied directly to programs requesting funding: 3.9 percent of the total agency income is designated for operating the Niles Hill residence.

Amount of grant request: $12,160
(Please note: The Allegany Arc is willing to contribute an in-kind labor contribution of $13,625.)

Specific project info: Please see narrative.

Project budget: Please see attached narrative; project budget attached.

NILES HILL IRA PROJECT
ALLEGANY ARC
240 O'CONNOR STREET
WELLSVILLE, NEW YORK 14895
(716) 593-5700
CONTACT: MARGARET WINANS

PROJECT OVERVIEW

It is the intent of Allegany Arc to provide additional living space for five (5) develop-mentally disabled individuals and year round pool access for physical therapy and range of motion for an additional 112 developmentally disabled individuals. This will be accomplished by renovating an existing garage at Arc's Niles Hill IRA (Individual Residential Alternative). Arc owns and occupies the house. The house is currently a permanent home for 5 developmentally disabled individuals. The project will also enclose an existing pool. Material costs for this renovation are estimated at $12,160. Arc's maintenance staff will provide the labor which is estimated at $13,625. Benefiting from this project are 117 individuals from Arc's six residences and four day program sites.

The house has a living room (10'x16'), dining room (9'x13'), kitchen (11'x12'), 3 bed-rooms (two are double occupancy) and a basement. The basement is not certified by OMRDD (Office of Mental Retardation and Developmental Disabilities) due to its layout and only having one exit. Because of physical limitations, consumers cannot access the basement. Thus, living space is very limited.

WORK TO BE COMPLETED

The garage is 432 square feet (18'x24'). It contains an 8'x10' laundry space where consumers do their laundry. The proposed project will renovate the remaining 352 square feet of space into a living/recreation area. (Please see the attached sketch.) The garage is connected to the house, the pool enclosure will connect to the garage. This will allow complete indoor access to the pool, so it can be used year round.

The pool, as seen on the sketch, has concrete already surrounding it. This will make enclosing it much easier and less expensive. The 20'x40' pool will be enclosed by a 32'x54' wood structure with roof. A pool heater exists in the garage and will be used to heat the enclosed pool.

The existing overhead door in the front of the garage will be removed and replaced with a wall with an entry door and window. A door from the rear wall will be removed, the opening enclosed and a window will be added to the back wall. This door will be installed in the wall by the pool, between the windows that are already there. This will give access to the pool area. All exterior walls will be insulated and moisture resistant sheet rock will be installed where needed. A wall mounted, forced air heater will be installed. Electric will be extended and new lights installed. All interior walls and wood will be primed and painted to match what exists.

The attached budget shows in detail the costs associated with completing this project. Maintenance staff, consisting of four (4), will provide the labor. They have carried out many projects similar to this and are very competent and capable of professionally completing this project. It is estimated that it will take approximately five (5) weeks to complete this work.

PROJECT NEED

Allegany Arc serves a diverse population of individuals. Many individuals are involved in some type of physical therapy or exercise program to assist them in gaining or maintaining some type of mobility or control. Aqua therapy or water aerobics are very beneficial to many of the consumers served by the Arc. Due to the inconsistent weather patterns in western New York, outdoor swimming is a limited activity as the water does not usually have an adequate chance to warm up enough for consistent swimming or exercise activities. A heated pool, which is in an enclosed area, would be most beneficial to consumers. Access to other pools is limited to day/time of openings and consistency of use is impossible. For some individuals, flotation devices are the nearest they come to independence without someone having to hold them or support them in some way. The weightlessness they experience in the water provides them with a freedom that people dependent on wheelchairs rarely experience!

A total of 117 developmentally disabled individuals served by Allegany Arc will benefit from enclosure of the pool. Of these, 55 individuals live permanently in the six (6) residences owned and operated by Allegany Arc.

Attached is specific information on 18 of the 55 individuals living in Arc residences. As you will note, most of them are in dire need of water therapy due to their physical conditions. Without this exercise regime, many will lose all or most range of motion (ROM) abilities and thus, require even more care. This can be reduced and perhaps prevented with water therapy. Maintaining independence is key to each and every one of us. It gives us the desire to keep trying and to go on living. Self-sufficiency is important in keeping these individuals as independent as possible. Giving these individuals the opportunity for water therapy will give them a new chance at fully enjoying life.

Some of the others in Arc day programs who will reap great benefits from an enclosed, heated pool are:

> Laura — exercise, movement, strengthening of legs and ankles (without stress on joints)

> Paul — out of wheelchair for freedom of movement

> Ida — exercise with weightlessness to prevent knee stress

Terry — out of wheelchair, freedom and fun

Martin — out of wheelchair, less stress on back

(Five individuals benefit.)

Seniors — gaining or maintaining mobility:

Barb, Bob, Fred, Austin, Jim, Eileen, Virginia, Don, Roy, Elizabeth, John, Patty, John, Don, Ron, Sandy, Mary, Shirley.

(Eighteen individuals benefit.)

Individuals involved in the TBI program would benefit as water therapy is utilized for enhanced movement in individuals with traumatic brain injury. They are:

John, Chad, Jay — These individuals use wheelchairs or canes to support them.

(Three individuals benefit.)

Social, safety, leadership and sportsmanship skills may also be practiced while having fun. Many individuals would benefit from all of these activities entwined in a regular exercise program. They include:

Judy, Eric, Terry, Tom, Marcy, Janice, Sharlene, Patty, Maureen, Brett, Chris, Holly, Lori, Frank, Jerry, Elizabeth, Jeanne, Marilyn, Doris, Cathy, Sarah, Mike, Rick, Lois, John, Robert, Dominick, Ann Jeanette, Michelle, Lisa, Chuck, Lynne, Mike, Diane, Phil, Carole.

(Thirty-seven individuals benefit.)

Benefits may also be derived from the standpoint of sensory input such as warm water, weightlessness, splashing, waterplay, etc. The indoor pool will be a great benefit to many people. Many consumers have expressed their enjoyment of pool use and wish it was easier to access. The only existing pool available to consumers is the one at the local school. It is very difficult to access, given the demand by the general public and the school itself. There are also restrictions on times that it is available.

The individuals listed above not only have developmental disabilities, but face many other physical challenges as well. Those in wheelchairs need the freedom of water to stay agile and to experience the rarity of being independent of their chair. Others have back, leg, neck, arm, etc. injuries that water therapy would greatly help. Many others are elderly, overweight, or otherwise limited in mobility. Water allows greater, less stressful body movements that are of significant benefit. Many see physical therapists who strongly recommend water therapy as ideal and the most beneficial form of treatment/exercise.

PROPOSED NILES HILL PROJECT

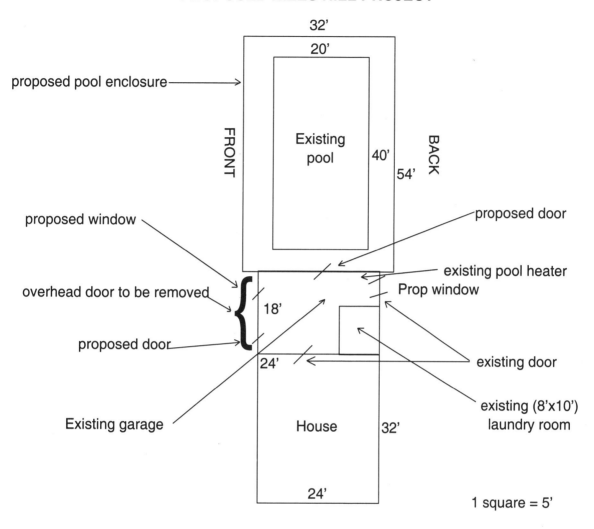

NILES HILL IRA RENOVATION BUDGET

$432.00	108-2x4x8	$291.00	35-sheet rock
$480.00	20-2x4x16	$101.00	insulation
$4,000.00	40' truss	$130.00	2-door locks
$1,200.00	6 windows	$40.00	32-2x4x8
$1,625.00	65 sheets plywood	$462.00	2-doors
$546.00	21 square shingles	$400.00	2- windows
$40.00	felt paper	$228.00	10-sheet /8 T-1-11
$70.00	3" screws (5000)	$1,652.00	Total garage renovation
$65.00	1⅝" screws (5000)		
$50.00	roof nails		
$2,000.00	misc.		
$1,652.00	garage renovation		
$12,160.00	Total materials		
$13,625.00	labor (in-house)		
$25,785.00	Grand total		

INDIVIDUALS TO BE SERVED BY PROPOSED ARC PROJECT

Laura
Diagnosis: Downs syndrome, profound MR, CP, Prader-Willi, obesity, uses a walker.

Laura needs exercise to strengthen her muscles for walking. She is also obese (196 lbs.) and swimming would be beneficial towards weight loss. The regular use of a pool would reduce the likelihood of fractures and sprains which she has been prone to by increasing her muscle strength and flexibility.

She should do a regular program of 1/2 hour at least three times a week in the pool.

Barbara
Diagnosis: Severe MR, CP, Bilateral hallux valgus & flat feet and uses a walker.

As Barb has gotten older her balance and strength have diminished. She has had to start using a walker. Regular strength training and exercise swimming would help her balance and increase flexibility.

She should do a regular program at least 1/2 hour 2 or 3 times a week in the pool.

David
Diagnosis: Profound MR, seizure disorder, CP, talpes valgus bilaterally, uses a walker.

David has a very unsteady gait which makes him very unsure on his feet even when using the walker. Exercise to improve flexibility and muscle strength would be of great benefit to him to prevent the many falls he has due to these problems.

I would recommend 1/2 hour at least 2 times a week in the pool.

Paul
Diagnosis: Moderate MR, CP with right hemiparesis including right arm, spasticity, scoliosis, seizure disorder, bilateral knee contractures, uses a wheelchair.

Paul has contractures of both knees and his right hand. Doing ROM exercises while in a weightless environment such as a pool would increase his flexibility and strength and prevent further contractures.

I would recommend 1/2 hour 2 times a week in the pool.

Albert
Diagnosis: Myotonic Dystrophy, cor Pulmonale, arthritis of left foot, Diabetes Mellitus, Moderate MR, uses a Bi-Pap machine at night and Oxygen prn.

Albert has a definite need for exercise. But as his breathing tolerance is limited the weightlessness of a pool would be very beneficial. He needs to build muscle strength and flexibility in his joints.

I would recommend 1/2 hour 2 or 3 times a week in the pool.

James

Diagnosis: Moderate MR, CP with spasticity in all extremities, severe kyphoscoliosis and arthritis, uses a wheelchair as refuses to ambulate due to stiffness and pain. History of spinal fractures, osteoporosis and foot deformities.

This man is supposed to do ROM and ambulate as much as possible but refuses to do so because of the pain and stiffness. The weightlessness of a pool would be very soothing to his arthritic joints as well as increasing his muscle strength and especially flexibility. The exercise is also needed to encourage ambulation which in turn will help reduce the opportunity for fractures from the osteoporosis.

I would recommend ½ hour 3 times a week or more as he can tolerate, full ROM in the pool.

Roy

Diagnosis: Profound MR, Seizure disorder, controlled glaucoma, scoliosis of upper dorsal spine, shorter right leg status post fracture and contracture of the left knee.

Roy ambulates but not without difficulty. He has a lot of stiffness and takes medication for arthritis pain. His spinal condition prevents him from standing straight or hyperextending his head and neck. He enjoys being busy and thus makes himself stay mobile and ambulate. Pool ROM would be of great benefit to relieve further contractures and increase flexibility in his spine.

I would recommend ½ hour for 2 times a week as he can tolerate.

Ida

Diagnosis: Severe MR, mixed personality disorder, Degenerative joint disease in knees, especially left knee, Pagets disease in left femur and hip and obesity.

Ida is obese, weighing about 196 lbs. She has a lot of pain in her knees which are also unstable. She will fall easily as a result. The Paget's disease requires gentle exercise which will help to prevent further deterioration. The weightlessness of swimming would be of great benefit to her knees and left femur and hip and would enable her to strengthen the muscles as well as improve her flexibility.

I would recommend she do ROM and gentle exercises for ½ hour 2 or 3 times a week in the pool.

Terry

Diagnosis: Severe MR, CP, Epilepsy, spastic quadriplegia and right hemiparesis, uses a wheelchair, is not able to ambulate alone but is able to crawl on hands and feet.

Terry needs regular ROM to prevent contractures and improve strength in his legs and back.

I would recommend ½ hour of pool exercise and ROM 2 times a week.

Robbin

Diagnosis: Severe MR, inactive seizure disorder, CP with right-sided spastic hemiplegia, she wears a short leg brace on the right side and a splint to her right hand at night due to contractures.

Robbin should have regular ROM to her right hand and legs to prevent further contractures.

I recommend ½ hour 2 times a week in the pool.

Minette

Diagnosis: Mild to Moderate MR, anxiety disorder and mania, arthritis of the left leg and foot and varicose veins. She uses a wheelchair and a walker.

ROM to the left leg and foot would help maintain flexibility and muscle tone. The pool would be a comfortable place for her to do this but access to and from the pool would be another problem. Either a ramp into the pool or a hydraulic lift would be needed.

I would recommend ½ hour 2 to 3 times a week as she can tolerate, in the pool doing ROM and gentle exercise.

Martin

Diagnosis: Severe MR, quadriparesis, severe kyphoscoliosis of dorsal lumbar spine, spasticity of lower extremities, right wrist contracture.

Martin needs regular ROM to maintain present abilities. He needs to maintain flexibility and increase strength to the extremities.

I would recommend ½ hour ROM and gentle exercise in the pool at least once a day. Twice a day would be better if his skin is not bothered by that much exposure to the water.

Ernest

Diagnosis: Severe MR. Suffered a CVA in 2/97 with resulting right-sided weakness noted mostly in arm and hand strength though some unsteadiness is seen in the right leg too.

Ernie has been attending OT to try and regain the strength in his right hand and arm. He also still had some weakness in the right leg but is walking without difficulty most of the time.

I would recommend ½ hour of ROM in the pool and other gentle exercise to strengthen and encourage flexibility in the right hand, arm and leg.

Lois

Diagnosis: Severe MR, CP with right hemiparesis and dense spastic hemiparesis in her upper extremity. Lower extremity is also slightly spastic.

Lois has an awkward gait. She has right hand contracture and wears a splint at night. She should have ROM at least 2 times a day to maintain full flexibility of the right arm.

I would recommend ½ hour 2 times a week in the pool and ROM 2 times a day otherwise. She could use the pool more often if she wished.

Jennie

Diagnosis: Moderate MR, CP, with spastic quadriplegia and resulting left-sided weakness and hypertension. She uses a wheelchair.

Jennie is fairly active in her chair but has very limited use of her hands. She should have ROM to all the contracted areas (hands, etc.) 2 times a day.

I would recommend ROM, reaching, etc. exercises suggested by PT be done 3 times a week in the pool.

Maureen

Diagnosis: Severe MR, CP with spastic quadriplegia with right-sided weakness, and a seizure disorder. Mo also uses a wheelchair.

Maureen needs regular ROM exercise to remain flexible and build strength. She has early contractures in her left arm, both hands and knees. She receives a muscle relaxant 2 times a day for spasticity.

I would recommend she receive ROM and other gentle exercise in the pool at least daily. She could go more often as long as her skin is not bothered. She should receive ROM at least 2 times a day total.

Brenda

Diagnosis: Profound MR, P.K.U., spastic quadriplegia, severe muscular atrophy of the lower extremities, osteoporosis. She uses a wheelchair but can walk with one assist for short distances.

Brenda needs to remain active and ROM to maintain flexibility to her legs and feet.

I would recommend she has ½ hour 2 or 3 times a week in the pool. She could go more often if she desired.

Jessie

Diagnosis: Profound MR, blindness, asymmetric spastic diplegia of the lower extremities and flexion contractures of the hips and knees. Decreased circulation of lower extremities due to lack of mobility, venous stasis, seizure disorder. She uses a wheelchair.

Jessie should have ROM to all extremities 2 times a day. This will prevent further deterioration but will not improve her present abilities. She has early contractures of both hands also.

I would recommend ROM and gentle exercise in the pool at least once a day if she can tolerate it. The water temperature must be considered due to her circulation problems. Also she will be very difficult to get in and out of the pool without a lift or a ramp.

Friends of Allegany County ARC Board of Directors

Board Title	Name	Address	Phone Number
President	Anne Torrey	2 Whitney Valley Ext. Road Almond, NY 14804	Home: (607) 276-6011
Vice President	Gladys Ackerman	19 N. Brooklyn Ave. Wellsville, NY 14895	Home: (716) 593-2101
Sec./Treasurer	Richard Witkowski	240 O'Connor St. Wellsville, NY 14895	Work: (716) 593-5700
Board Member	Dr. Albert Vanderlinde	261 N. Main St. Wellsville, NY 14895	Home: (716) 593-5828
Board Member	Joseph Tripodi	4192-A Bolivar Road Wellsville, NY 14895	Work: (716) 593-4400
Board Member	Carolyn Burrell	Stannards Road Wellsville, NY 14895	Work: (716) 593-4038
Board Member	Mary Good	1669 County Route 22 Whitesville, NY 14897	Home: (607) 356-3537

ALLEGANY COUNTY CHAPTER NYSARC, INC.
For the 1998-1999 Year

BOARD OF DIRECTORS

OFFICERS

PRESIDENT
Eugene Krumm
19 Pine St., Apt. 14
Wellsville, NY 14895
(716) 593-3937 HOME

VICE-PRESIDENT
Thomas Talbett, Jr.*
Box 167-A
Friendship, NY 14739
(716) 593-4200, Ext. 322 WORK
(716) 973-2223 HOME

TREASURER
Linda Clayson*
3133 Knights Creek Road
Scio, NY 14880
(716) 593-1500, Ext. 232 WORK
(716) 593-6853 HOME

SECRETARY
Kevin Gildner
255 Proctor Road
Wellsville, NY 14895
(716) 593-2341 WORK
(716) 593-7417 HOME

MEMBERS

Khalid Ashraf, Ph.D.
174 N. Main St.
Alfred, NY 14802
(607) 587-4191 WORK
(607) 587-8867 HOME
(607) 587-4714, Mssg. w/Secretary
(607) 587-4263, Fax

Ruthann McCarthy*
20 Madison St.
Wellsville, NY 14895
(716) 593-4830 WORK

Amy Rummel, Ph.D.*
6205 Burt Hill Road
Canisteo, NY 14823
(607) 871-2295 WORK
(607) 698-2681 HOME

Jody Torrey*
183 E. Dyke St.
Wellsville, NY 14895

Nicholas DiBiase*
3437 Center Drive, Riverview Heights
Wellsville, NY 14895
(716) 593-7247 HOME

Patricia Ricketts
P.O. Box 14, Claybed Road
Hume, NY 14745
(716) 567-2251 WORK
(716) 567-2765 HOME

James Stevens
3152 Riverside Drive
Wellsville, NY 14895
(716) 593-1612 HOME

*Denotes blood relative

Fact Sheet

Allegany Arc
a resource & career opportunity center

. . . was formed in 1961 by a small group of parents determined to give their children with disabilities a better life.

Allegany Arc, a resource & career opportunity center's mission states —
The Allegany Arc is dedicated to providing opportunities to people with special needs and their families that will assist in improving the quality of their lives. As an advocate, the Arc will provide support and services ensuring each person the opportunity to learn, achieve, contribute and lead.

The Allegany Arc is comprised of several divisions, each containing numerous programs.

❑ Rehabilitation/Clinical Division:

PWI Rehabilitation
> work skills training
> vocational evaluations
> personal adjustment training
> life skills training

Service Coordination
> provides advocacy
> intake services

Other Programs
> Wee Steps Preschool Evaluation Program
> Nursing

❑ Community Services Division:

Day Habilitation
> teaches everyday living skills
> senior citizens' program
> recreation/social activities

Family Support Services
> respite
> crisis intervention
> family care
> outreach/prevention
> family reimbursement

Other programs
> at-home residential habilitation
>> teaches living and safety skills in the home environment
> Horizons — Consumer Direct Personal Assistance Program
> Guardianship
> Traumatic Brain Injury Program (TBI)

ALLEGANY ARC
1997 REVENUES

	REVENUES	%
SALES	788,025	11.7%
OMH	103,273	1.5%
OMRDD	4,808,169	71.6%
VESID	198,684	3.0%
OTHER	776,069	11.6%
FUNDRAISING	44,055	0.7%
TOTAL	6,718,275	99.3%

*Percentages may not total due to rounding.

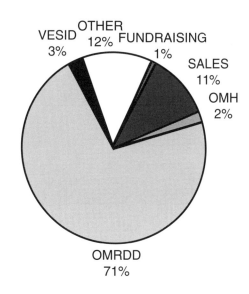

TOTAL INCOME	6,718,275	
FUNDRAISING INCOME	44,055	0.7% OF INCOME
NILES RESIDENTIAL INCOME	260,351	3.9% OF INCOME
TOTAL ADMIN O/H	537,390	8.0% OF INCOME
FUNDRAISING ADMIN O/H	2,085	0.4% OF ADMIN O/H

1998 BUDGET FOR NILES HILL RESIDENCE

REVENUES:

PARTICIPANT FEES	47,284*
OMRDD FUNDING	249,501**
TOTAL REVENUES	296,785

EXPENSES:

PERSONAL SERVICES	159,089
FRINGE BENEFITS	36,775
GENERAL OPERATING	52,088
PROPERTY & EQUIP. DEP.	26,054
ADMIN O/H	22,779
TOTAL EXPENSES	296,785

BALANCED BUDGET	0

Niles Residence houses five individuals (vacancy factor included)
 *1787 DAYS @ $26.46/DAY
**1787 DAYS @ $139.62/DAY

5 Winning Grants From Federal Agencies

The federal grantmaking process begins long before you ever submit a single piece of paper to a federal agency. Federal grant programs originate with the enactment of authorizing legislation by Congress and the president. The programs are then funded through annual appropriations bills passed by Congress.

Authorizing legislation creates the program, establishing its goals, eligibility, allowable activities, administrative procedures and other guiding information. In most instances, a separate *appropriations* bill must also be passed to actually provide the funding for the program.

Understanding the difference between an authorizing law and an appropriations law is very important because even if Congress creates a new program, there is no guarantee the program will have funding to make awards to grantseekers. Quite often the media will report on new programs that Congress has created. In most cases, however, those programs must wait up to one year before Congress actually appropriates funds to allow the programs to operate. You do not want to waste your time and money preparing a proposal for a program that has yet to be (or never will be) funded.

Once Congress has authorized and funded a program, the federal agency charged with administering the initiative must develop procedures for soliciting and reviewing applications, selecting grantees, distributing funds and monitoring the program. With the federal government's current mindset of reducing the paperwork burden on grantees, offices are trying to reduce the amount of rules and regulations attached to grant programs. Increasingly they are relying on the authorizing legislation to define how grant programs will be administered. Therefore, grantseekers must also be aware of a program's authorizing legislation.

What Kind of Funding Is Available From the Federal Government?

Successful grantseekers understand the different types of funding available from the federal government: *entitlement funds, formula grants* and *discretionary grants.*

➢ **Entitlement funds** are awarded to all entities that qualify for assistance under a program's statutory requirements. This category of funding includes programs such as Medicare and the welfare program known as Temporary Assistance for Needy Families. Entitlement fund programs are not subject to the federal government's annual appropriations process; the funding is considered "mandatory."

➢ **Formula grant programs**, like entitlement programs, award funds to all eligible entities. Allocations are based on factors specified by the program's authorizing legislation, such as the poverty rate in a given area, the number of individuals served by the program or the total population. Congress decides each year as part of the appropriations process how much funding will be provided for formula grant programs.

Typically, formula and entitlement funds are awarded to states, which in turn make "subgrants" to eligible local agencies and organizations. These subgrants may be made on the basis of a formula mandated by law or on a competitive basis. The procedures for local agencies and private nonprofit organizations that are seeking subgrants of federal funds from a state will vary by program and by state.

If you are interested in a state subgrant, you should first check the program's authorizing legislation to determine whether your organization is eligible and if your proposed project fits within the program's scope.

Because each state is responsible for distributing its funds, local groups must look to their state capital, not Washington, D.C., for information and guidelines on receiving subgrants of federal funds.

> ➤ **Discretionary grants,** unlike formula or entitlement grants, are awarded through a competitive process. Proposals are reviewed and ranked according to the federal program's authorizing legislation and any regulations that have been established by the administrative agency. This review process gives each agency the discretion to determine which applicants best address the program's requirements and goals, and are, therefore, most worthy of funding.

Discretionary funds are awarded directly from the federal government to the grantee organization – not to the state (although in many instances, states may be eligible for competitive discretionary grants). As it does with the other types of federal aid programs, Congress creates discretionary grant programs through authorizing legislation and funds them through annual appropriations bills.

Most organizations that want to receive federal funding will be competing for discretionary grants.

In this chapter, you will find information about how the federal government announces competitions for discretionary grants, the application process and tips on how to win federal discretionary grants.

How Discretionary Grants Are Solicited

Knowing when and where the federal government announces that it is accepting applications for discretionary grants is a key in finding financial assistance for your organization's projects and services. A limited number of federal programs accept applications on an ongoing basis; the vast majority of agencies issue special notices of funding availability (NOFAs). A NOFA will include specific information on a program's purpose, eligibility requirements, application deadline and other pertinent requirements and procedures.

Federal agencies will also announce any program priorities through the NOFA. For each competition, the agency may specify a type of project, eligible entity, subject matter or population that it will consider funding. In some cases, applicants will be required to address these priorities; in other instances, those who address them will receive special consideration during the proposal review process.

For example, a U.S. Department of Housing and Urban Development program that offers funds for community development initiatives may award additional review points to applicants that serve extremely high-poverty communities. Under another program competition, the Education Department may establish a priority that requires all applicants to provide services to parents of children with a specific type of disability. In either instance, if your proposal does not address this priority, it will not even be considered for funding.

Unfortunately, because of the nature of the federal government, it is difficult to say exactly when discretionary grant programs will be open for competition. Federal agencies must wait for Congress and the White House to complete work on the annual appropriations bills before they can begin awarding money under any competitive grant program. If lawmakers are on schedule, agencies may start accepting applications early in the federal government's fiscal year, which runs from Oct. 1 to Sept. 30.

However, if fights over the federal budget delay the appropriations process – which has been the case in most recent years – the timeline for soliciting grant applications and awarding funds can be uncertain.

Therefore it is important for grantseekers to know where to look for federal grant announcements.

Where to Look for Federal Grant Opportunity Announcements

The majority of federal funding opportunities are announced in the *Federal Register*, the government's official daily publication listing agency rules and announcements. Federal agencies also frequently post application information on their World Wide Web sites. *(See Chapter 8, Resources, for more information on how to find out about federal funding opportunities.)*

Keep in mind, however, that publications such as the *Federal Register* do not always completely describe funding opportunities and the grants application process. The *Federal Register* is primarily meant to notify the public of program deadlines, priorities and basic goals, as well as the application procedure. Grantseekers must always obtain a complete application packet – available from the administering federal agency – before submitting an application.

Further, you should know that in instances where the program is restricted to a certain geographic area or certain eligible entities, the federal government may communicate directly with potential grantees, rather than announcing the program in the *Federal Register*.

Formula and entitlement programs, as described earlier, are typically handled in this manner. If your agency or organization is interested in receiving a subgrant through such a program, check with the state agency responsible for administering the federal program to learn more about applying for a subgrant.

In addition, for some programs, the federal administering agency will maintain a list of interested, or qualified organizations and automatically send them application information when it becomes available. You should contact the agency administering any program in which you are interested to find out if they maintain such a list.

Tips for Federal Grantseekers

Once you have decided to apply for federal funding, what can you do to help improve your chances of winning support? Like all grantmakers, the federal government looks for proposals that adhere to the basics of good proposal writing – clarity, well-defined goals and methods, accurate information, a well thought–out evaluation plan and budget accountability.

Further, federal officials say many proposals are not even considered because they do not meet basic program requirements. Do not waste your time or money applying for a grant that is not right for you.

One of the first things you should do in deciding whether to apply for a grant is make sure that your organization is eligible to receive funding under the program in which you are interested. Eligibility requirements are drawn from the program's authorizing statute, but you should also carefully read the NOFA. If you are not sure whether your organization qualifies for funding, contact a program official. *(Note: Program officers will want to know the specific program title and may also ask for the program's Catalog of Federal Domestic Assistance (CFDA) number as discussed in Chapter 8, Resources. Be sure you have this information before calling with any questions about a particular program.)*

You may also want to review any regulations that apply to the program. The federal government's *Code of Federal Regulations* (CFR) is a compilation of current general and program-specific rules and regulations. You should obtain a copy of the relevant section of the CFR to guide you in your grantseeking and proposal writing efforts. Each program's NOFA will indicate what sections of the CFR are applicable. However, the CFR is updated only once a year and therefore may not have all of the current program regulations. Complete information about program regulations will be included in the application packet.

For more information about the CFR, contact the U.S. Government Printing Office, Superintendent of Documents, Mail Stop SSOP, Washington, DC 20402-9328; (202) 512-1800; **http://www.access.gpo.gov.**

You can also obtain assistance from the federal agency when you are trying to fill out your application. Most application packages include detailed instructions on how to fill out the forms and write the required program description. In addition, many agencies offer technical assistance via telephone or e-mail contact with program staff, or through regional workshops for potential applicants. You will find information about technical assistance in the program's NOFA or in the application packet.

Complete application packets are available from program officers and are sometimes included in the *Federal Register* NOFA or posted on the program agency's Web site.

Serving as a Field Reader

One way to gain insight into the federal government's grantmaking process is to volunteer as a field reader, or proposal reviewer, for a federal grants competition.

Program offices sometimes solicit nominations from experts and practitioners who are willing to serve on independent panels that evaluate and score the requests for funding that have been submitted under a specific program competition. Notices seeking field readers are often published in professional magazines and newsletters, as well as in federal publications such as the *Federal Register*.

Individuals interested in serving as field readers must have extensive experience in their profession or in the grant program area, and must be willing to commit a great deal of time and energy to the review process. In some instances, reviewers may be asked to spend as much as a week evaluating grant proposals. Additionally, keep in mind that some federal agencies will mail applications to reviewers, but others may require that reviewers travel to a central location. Reviewers who are convened as a panel in one location to judge applications are typically reimbursed for their expenses on a per diem basis.

However, if you are selected as a field reader, the experience can be invaluable. It gives you the opportunity to see first-hand the differences in quality and concept among the proposals. It also gives you the chance to learn about the behind-the-scenes process of federal grantmaking and to gather information about successful – as well as unsuccessful – applications.

Another benefit of serving as a field reader is that you will have the opportunity to develop personal relationships with federal program staff. Having contacts within program offices can make it easier to get advice and information when you are writing your own grant proposal.

A Model Federal Program

As discussed in Chapter 2, *Beginning the Grantseeking Process*, looking at successful proposals submitted by other organizations can be a good way of helping you improve your own grantwriting skills.

On the following pages, you will find the narrative description of a project that was funded under the Education Department's 21st Century Community Learning Centers program. The program provides discretionary grants to public elementary and secondary schools in inner-city and rural areas for the operation of school-based learning centers. The centers provide educational, recreational, social and health services to students, their parents and the community at large during non-school hours.

The program's authorizing legislation lists 13 types of activities that may be supported and requires grantees to provide at least four activities. In addition to the narrative, applicants requesting funding under this program were required to complete the standard forms required from all organizations seeking financial assistance from the federal government – Standard Forms 424, 424A, 424B, 424C, 424D, LLL, and Certification Regarding Debarment, Suspension, Ineligibility and Voluntary Exclusion - Lower Tier Covered Transactions. (*See Chapter 7*, Forms, *for more information on these forms.*)

All proposals submitted for this program were reviewed by an independent panel – not Education Department officials – composed of three outside experts. Proposals were rated on a 100-point scale, with the highest-ranked proposals being recommended for funding. The criteria used to judge applications were:

> ➤ need for the project (30 points). The extent to which the project would provide services or otherwise address the needs of students at risk of educational failure.

> ➤ quality of the project design (30 points). The extent to which the goals, objectives and outcomes to be achieved are clearly specified and measurable; the extent to which the design of the project is appropriate, and will successfully address, the needs of the target population; and the extent to which the project would establish linkages with other appropriate agencies and organizations to provide services.

> ➤ adequacy of resources (15 points). The adequacy of the support, including facilities, equipment, supplies and other resources, from the applicant organizations or the lead applicant; and the extent to which the costs are reasonable in relation to the number of persons to be served and to the anticipated results and benefits.

> ➤ quality of the management plan (15 points). The adequacy of the management plan to achieve the objectives of the proposed project on time and within the budget, including clearly defined responsibilities, timelines and milestones for accomplishing project tasks; and how the applicant will ensure that a diversity of perspectives are brought to bear in the operation of the project, including those of parents, teachers, the business community, a variety of disciplinary and professional fields, recipients or beneficiaries, or others as appropriate.

> ➤ quality of project evaluation (10 points). The extent to which the methods of evaluation include the use of objective performance measures that are clearly related to the intended outcomes of the project and will produce quantitative and qualitative data.

In addition, projects that were designed to assist students in meeting or exceeding state and local standards in core academic subjects such as reading and mathematics received an additional five points under a competitive priority established by the department.

A program official said that while she could not comment on the specific qualities of a particular project, she said one of the keys to a successful project is to address *all* of the requirements indicated in the application packet and to tie the proposal together in a way that shows your program will work.

Said another program official, "My advice in one sentence is for applicants to ask, 'Does it sound like the project will work?' We look at the project as a whole. Does it make sense? Can they do what they are proposing to do?"

Bayfield Public Schools

Project Proposal: 21st Century Community Learning Centers

THE LIGHTHOUSE PROJECT: Learning is a Community Affair

The Bayfield School District, established in 1896, is a public school district located in extreme northern Wisconsin with a total K–12 enrollment of 518 students. We operate elementary, middle and high schools at a K–12 facility in the city of Bayfield and an elementary school at LaPointe, separated from the mainland by the waters of Lake Superior. Bayfield is a remote district, with a geographic area of over 250 square miles, giving us a ratio of only two students per square mile. The district serves families in the city of Bayfield and four rural townships, which encompass the Red Cliff Indian Reservation and Madeline Island. Our community has very high poverty rates with 65 percent of our students eligible for free or reduced–price meals during the 1997/1998 school term. Bayfield School students and staff compose a multicultural community of learners with 63 percent of students being Native American.

Too high a percentage of Bayfield students in grades four to nine fall more than one year behind grade level in basic academic skills. Data analysis indicates that the decline in achievement skill levels begins at about grade four and accelerates through grade seven with some continuing breakdown in absence from school, failing grades, conduct rule infractions and students dropping out of school are the result. Risk factors for children and adolescents in the Bayfield community are many including: cultural and personal isolation, alcohol and other drug use as a community norm, and a high percentage of single parent families.

These risk factors create a variety of needs among community members. An active response is called for to meet these needs of youth and adults alike. Proposed 21st Century Center elements of integrated education, health, social service, recreational and cultural programs, literacy education, expanded library service hours, telecommunications and technology education for individuals of all ages, and parenting skills education programs will help move Bayfield forward. This project will place special emphasis on meeting the needs of early and late adolescents. 21st Century Center resources will provide much needed help to create a new, self sustaining set of understandings and skills for an improvement of the quality of life of all the community's citizenry.

The proposed program has two major goals: first, to advance the academic and educational skill and attainment of all participants; and, second, to connect skill competence developed through education to vocations and the world of productive work. To accomplish these goals the project plans to use the Wisconsin Model Academic Standards, The Wisconsin Resilient Learner Model of Comprehensive Services, the Iowa Safe Communities Project materials and the Mid–Continent Regional Educational Laboratory "Compendium of Standards and Benchmarks for K–12 Education."

- NEED FOR PROJECT -

1) APPLICANT / ORGANIZATION OVERVIEW

The Bayfield School District, established in 1896, is a public school district located in extreme northern Wisconsin with a total K–12 enrollment of 518 students. We operate elementary, middle, and high schools at a K–12 facility in the city of Bayfield and an elementary school at LaPointe, separated from the mainland by the waters of Lake Superior. Bayfield is a remote district, with a geographic area of over 250 square miles, giving us a ratio of only two students per square mile. The district serves families in the city of Bayfield and four rural townships, which encompass the Red Cliff Indian Reservation and Madeline Island. Our community has very high poverty rates with 65 percent of our students eligible for free or reduced-price meals during the 1997/1998 school term. Bayfield School students and staff compose a multicultural community of learners, with 63 percent of students being Native American.

Given the isolated nature of our district, and the fact that we operate two elementary schools, one of which is located on an island, our per-pupil costs rank high among state of Wisconsin public school districts. Notwithstanding our relatively high per-pupil costs, Bayfield is a "property poor" district with a significant portion of the school district area composed of U.S. managed lands (Apostle Islands National Lakeshore and the Red Cliff Indian Reservation). Thus, we have a high property tax-rate to support our necessarily high per-pupil expenditures.

2) RISK FACTORS / NEEDS OF STUDENTS AND COMMUNITY

Risk factors for children and adolescents in the Bayfield school community include:
Cultural and personal isolation
Alcohol and other drug use as a community norm
Teen pregnancy
High percentage of single parent families
Physical and emotional abuse
Poor nutrition
Insufficient access to information resources
Lack of law enforcement availability
Lack of parenting skills
Lack of access to quality, supervised, recreational opportunities
Unavailability of transportation
Severity of climate

These issues have been identified through formal survey of students, school staff, tribal members, county service providers and local businesses in 1995 and through the community based process of developing the school district strategic plan. These factors affect children, adolescents and adults in a variety of forms. Children and adolescents suffer victimization by peers, exposure to illegal drug use and alcohol, excess absence from school, marginal health, diminished academic achievement and ambivalence about their hopes for the future. Adults experience severe stress from economic issues, poor health and difficulty in providing for the needs of their families. Educational attainment of the children suffers. Longitudinal analysis of student group achievement test scores, report card grades, scores on third grade reading tests, review of weekly academic deficiency lists, student attendance lists, along with Title I achievement test scores and enrollments and numerous interviews with children individually and in small groups point to serious risk for healthy personal development and academic attainment.

Too high a percentage of Bayfield students in grades four to nine fall more than one year behind grade level in basic academic skills. Data analysis of grades one through nine indicates that the decline in achievement levels and grades begins at about grade four and accelerates through grade seven with some continuing breakdown in student skill and achievement occurring through grade nine. Excess student absence from school is an associated occurrence with other problems including failing grades. Further, study of Bayfield high school students who become seriously credit deficient in high school indicates that the pattern of academic skill deficit and subsequent credit deficiency are linked to dropping out of school. The pattern is particularly clear in examination of ninth grade credit standings. Students who finish high school freshman year with three or fewer credits are at very high risk to become drop outs from school.

3) PROJECT RESPONSE TO STUDENT AND COMMUNITY NEEDS

PROPOSED PROJECT ELEMENTS
The following components constitute this project:

Integrated education, health, social service, recreational and cultural programs

Literacy Education Programs

Expanded library service hours to serve community needs

Nutrition and health programs

Telecommunications and technology education programs for individuals of all ages

Parenting skills education programs

Summer and weekend school programs in conjunction with recreation programs

Services for individuals with disabilities

Services for individuals who leave school before graduating from secondary school, regardless of the age of such individual

All of these project elements will be available at each of the two proposed Community Learning Centers, the school facilities at Bayfield and at LaPointe on Madeline Island. The entire program will be available to one hundred percent of the students and family members of the Bayfield Public School District including children who are enrolled at the Holy Family Parochial School and those children who participate in a "home school." **The program has two major goals: to advance the academic and educational skill and attainment of all participants; and to connect skill competence developed through education to vocations and the world of productive work.** This will be accomplished within a safe, drug- and violence-free atmosphere where children and adults can explore their potentials and learn specific ways these potentials connect to lifelong education and the workplace.

Program elements provide the opportunity for each student and family to develop within themselves new resources enhancing personal resilience and, thereby, success in meeting the challenges they each face daily. Each program element, then, is chosen and is important to accomplishing the project goals by diminishing a specific risk factor(s) through meeting an associated need.

4) STATUS OF PRESENT PROGRAMS

A) Current Offerings

The Bayfield School District maintains a number of program initiatives which focus on promoting the health and safety of students. The district integrates Human Growth and Development education into the curriculum of kindergarten through grade 12. The sequence of instruction includes nine elements with safety, drugs and alcohol and healthy living each in a specific component of the curriculum at each grade level. The curriculum is written and school board approved and is taught in every classroom at the school. These efforts are reinforced with mandated health classes taught to all grade seven and 10 students and several lyceum presentations during the year by special events presenters. The Bayfield School District has actively organized and implemented a variety of AODA education program elements following the State of Wisconsin model for comprehensive programs and U.S. Drug–Free Schools guidelines. Conflict resolution skills are taught in a nine week sequence to all students in grades kindergarten through eight as part of the developmental guidance curriculum. Students are taught "Peace Education" at the kindergarten to grade eight levels in a regular, systematic and recurring fashion. American Indian history and culture are taught in all grades at the Bayfield school focusing upon traditional values of respect for other persons, honorable living and community faithfulness.

The schools have teacher aides at the elementary grades and two part time tutors at the high school level. The role of these personnel is to help students improve their academic skill. The school district employs a full time home/school coordinator and the Red Cliff tribe funds an academic resource coordinator for grades nine to 12. The school provides a full range of Exceptional Education resources for students with disabilities through employment of needed special educators and support services specialists. These services are coordinated in the schools by two Pupil Services Teams, one for students in the elementary and middle schools and one for the high school grades. While these resources are effective and beneficial, there is a profound contrast between the support children have at school during the instructional day and the picture that greets them after the last bell rings.

B) Shortcomings and Gaps

In listening to students, they identify the hours immediately after school, the 3:30 to 5:30 p.m. period, as the time of the day when they often have no help with learning, organized recreation opportunities are limited or nonexistent and they are at the "mercy" of older neighborhood children and young adults. There is little or no opportunity for children to approach or access community based social services or health care resources. There is no regular coordination and integration of these services with education so that stable, timely access is available to the resources that each agency possesses to maximize benefits of the client. There is no regular parent skill development teaching being provided by any agency within the school district nor in adjacent communities of Washburn or Ashland. There is no systematic nutrition education available to young families in this entire area. There currently is no organized remedial learning, homework completion or academic skill building opportunity available to every child in the district. There is a small after school program for selected fourth through ninth grade students but it meets only three days each week and has had to reject numerous student applicants who wished to participate owing to the program's very limited financial resources. Another severe gap in community support is transportation for students which is nonexistent beyond what parents may be able to provide. This lack of transport service particularly effects elementary and middle school students who must depend on the school bus at 3:20 to get home. There is no alternative. This is a critical element because the rural dispersion of families in the district currently makes children absolutely dependent upon adult help to see friends, stay after school, visit a public library, play a game of football, or get involved in a community drama presentation.

Services for young adults and parents to diminish the burdens of lack of educational opportunity, lack of jobs and costs related to travel are very thinly spread. The nearest vocational college is a 65–mile round trip from Bayfield, the nearest Wisconsin Department of Vocational Rehabilitation Office with services for the disabled is a 160–mile round trip to Superior. Job information and counseling are not available in this community outside of the school counseling services, limited public library materials and occasional itinerant consulting services. This makes the use of information technology of paramount importance to the members of this community. It is imperative that people of all ages have the opportunity to learn about and access modern, computer based information resources for personal, educational and economic gain. The Bayfield School District has made a start with this process by making its modest number of computers available for adult education classes taught by knowledgeable business resource persons in the evening, but much more needs to be offered and accomplished. A recent written survey of Bayfield parents with children enrolled at school revealed that 82 percent would have their children participate in an after school program consisting of educational and avocational elements with most indicating it should last until 5:30 p.m.

- 21ST CENTURY PROGRAM OUTLINE -

1. STAFFING AND FACILITIES – Project Director, full time; 12 tutors/activity leaders, part time; and three public library based tutors, part time. Once every week a member of the staff from local Health offices, Social Services, Red Cliff Drug and Alcohol Treatment Center, Bayfield County 4H, and Bayfield County Youth Court will visit at the school and be available to staff, students and parents for consultation and occasional special presentations. They will assist with activities of the Centers as possible. The district currently has a facility use policy in place which states the rules and regulations applicable to building use and supervision guidelines.

2. ACTIVITIES –

A. Recreation: All students who choose to stay after school will participate in a 25 minute recreation period immediately after classes. This will consist of various skill games which focus upon group interaction and cooperative effort to master a challenging task. These activities will be led by tutor/activity leaders, take place in school or on adjacent playgrounds and be planned in advance. These will be aimed at fostering an appreciation of teamwork, mutual effort and expanding the childrens' physical skills.

B. Snack: There will be ten minutes following recreation for a daily snack consisting of a healthy item and include milk or fruit juice.

C. Academics:

1). Approximately 45 students in grades four through eight will make a commitment to attend on Monday, Tuesday, and Thursday of each school week. Student and their parent will sign an agreement pledging the child to participate for a full semester. The focus of their activities will be upon enhancing their learning skills using the University of Kansas Learning Strategies. The content of their learning will be academic skill materials from their grade levels. These students will be selected and recruited based on at-risk factors of below grade achievement, lack of regular school work completion, and low performance grades. These students will work in groups of seven students and meet with the same tutor for the semester.

2). Four tutor/activity leaders will be present five afternoons a week to assist students who signed up for a particular activity with homework completion before the "special event" to help students progress with particular school assignments. (Estimate 35–55 student participants)

D. Avocations: A list of activity opportunities will be posted two weeks in advance which students may sign up for and participate in as they become available. This set of activities will be built from a student survey of interests. They may include activities such as art, drama, puppet making, kayak use, swimming instruction, chess, creative writing, video tape creation, autobiographies, Great Books studies, and cultural studies like "myths and legends", etc. Another set of activities will be selected by leadership and include such offerings as cooking and healthy eating, conflict resolution skills, health topics of interest to children, drug and alcohol information, and healthy lifestyles issues. Another set of activities will be continuously available surrounding learning how to use the computer and the internet as a resource for learning. Tutors will guide student participation in these events. On occasion, resource people from the community will be involved when special knowledge, experience or skills are called for to successfully involve children.

E. Adult Literacy and Services for Individuals Not Graduated: EvenStart personnel will organize programs for adults that focus upon GED completion, reading improvement and family literacy skills. Extension courses will be offered locally at the Bayfield Community Learning Centers through cooperation with the Wisconsin Indianhead Technical College. Maximum use possible will be made of the NWCES Network which has distance learning studios at the Bayfield School, Indianhead Technical College and University of Wisconsin–Superior enabling two way interactive instruction. Also, an added part time staff person will be at each of the three public libraries in the school district to assist adults with finding educational resources and assist with job preparation and search materials including the use of the computer and the World Wide Web. This will be reinforced by the Cooperative Educational Service Area No. 12 (CESA No. 12) resource staff from the Northwest Career Information Center through staff training and direct service.

F. Parent Skills Education: A continuous parent support activity will be established at the schools to provide information resources to parents on various topics concerning child raising issues. Discussion groups will be scheduled in advance on a variety of topics of interest to moms and dads, grandparents, aunts and uncles.

G. Transportation: Students will be taken home each evening leaving school at approximately 5:30 p.m. Another opportunity to go home will be provided at 6:45 so that high school students can take maximum advantage of the school's after–school athletics program, do home work after practice at school, and then get home in a safe and timely manner.

H. Summer Session: There will be a two month, five day a week summer program which will provide a safe and fun recreational program with field trips and personal enhancement skill building. This community resource will operate for six hours each weekday and be free to district children. Children visiting the area with parents may sign up for this program daily for a fee. This program component will operate through the district Community Education department.

I. Educational Technology: The 21st Century Community Learning Centers will offer computer education classes on a continuous basis throughout the school year for all citizens. A modest fee will be charged and subsidized though project grant funds so that family finances are not a barrier to class participation. Topics such as basic computer operation, using a browser program to explore the internet, computers and word processing, and the use of the computer for e–mail are examples of the type of courses which will be offered. There will also be courses on the use of the internet for vocational learning and job finding. The district will also work to significantly enhance the use of the school district's distance learning resources (the NWCES Network) to offer courses relevant to job preparation, parent education, nutrition and other topics of interest to adult learners.

J. Services for Individuals with Disabilities: Health consultation, learning consultation and assistive technology services will be available to all community members who have a need for these resources. Health department partners, Wisconsin Department of Vocational Rehabilitation and school special education resources will all be available to assist individuals with disabilities to further their educations and career aspirations.

- QUALITY OF PROJECT SERVICES -

1) Strategies for Community Participation

The Bayfield School District student population is approximately sixty-five percent American Indian, most members of the Red Cliff Band of Chippewa. To be responsive to the character of the Indian culture and that of all Bayfield students, this project proposes to utilize the *Resilient Learner Model* outlined in the Wisconsin Department of Public Instruction publication "Wisconsin's Framework for Comprehensive School Health Programs." "The ultimate goal of the framework is to develop and support *healthy, resilient, successful learners* by helping organize programs, services and instruction into an integrated system." Several district personnel have received training in the use of the model. It is the basis for the Pupil Services Team organization that currently operates. It was chosen for this project because of the district's successful experience with it and, also, because it includes provision for strong Family and Community Connections which are an integral part of the American Indian way of life thereby helping to insure involvement by the largest number of community members possible. "Families are the primary prevention and youth development agents for their children." This model provides a framework for making the program elements culturally competent and thereby helping to assure equity and participation by all who have a need.

2) Services Impact

The Governor's Council on Model Academic Standards has recently published "Wisconsin's Model Academic Standards"; expectations for the attainment of every child attending a public school in the state. This was a collaborative effort by parents, businesses, educators and state agency representatives. These standards address language arts, science, math, and social studies. Included within as subtopics are media and technology, physical science and geography. There are specific grade level performance expectations for each of these topics. The Bayfield Schools 21st Century Learning Centers expect to boost and enhance every school age participants likelihood of meeting these educational standards. (Goal No. 1).

The Mid-continent Regional Educational Laboratory at Aurora, Colorado has published "Content Knowledge: A Compendium of Standards and Benchmarks for K-12 Education." The laboratory identifies standards for Life Skills relative to thinking and reasoning, self regulation and working with others. These standards are drawn from a variety of regional and national organizations, reported by grade level, and stated in clear, performance oriented language. These standards create a bridge connecting academic knowledge and skill to the circumstances and requirements of the workplace. They set specific expectations for successful performance in the workplace. The Bayfield Schools 21st Century Learning Centers expect to boost and enhance every school age participant's likelihood of meeting these educational benchmarks. (Goal No. 2).

University of Kansas is a leader in development and training in the use of learning strategies to improve student performance. These techniques for learning are validated in published research. "The use of learning strategies by low achievers enables them to perform at levels that are competitive with their normally achieving peers." The teachers acting as after school tutors in this project will all receive thorough training in the Learning Strategies. This will enable students to master new learning skills which directly affect their performance in daily classes. At-risk learners will have a powerful new tool which can be applied both in and out of school, not just one more review of material they did not master the first three times it was presented to them. They will learn how to learn more successfully. The Bayfield Schools 21st Century Learning Centers expect to boost and enhance every school age participant's learning readiness and resourcefulness and decrease drug use and violence through this Center's significantly expanded learning opportunities for children and youth. (Goals No. 1 and No. 2)

3) Collaboration

The following agencies and organizations helped in the planning of this project or have agreed to participate:

- *Red Cliff Tribe:* social services, Indian child welfare, community health services, Family Preservation and Support Project, the First Prevention AODA Center and Red Cliff AODA Prevention and Treatment Center.
- *Bayfield County:* Social Services Department, 4H Extension Service, County Youth Court, and County Health Department
- *Bayfield Business Community:* Trek & Trail, Big Water Learning Center, Bayfield Chamber of Commerce
- *Bayfield School:* Title I, Special Education, Community Education, Summer School Program, the Kayak Club
- *Cooperative Educational Service Agency No. 12:* (Intermediate School District) Center for Instruction and Evaluation, Center for Careers, Center for Technology

- QUALITY OF THE MANAGEMENT PLAN -

1) Staffing and Leadership Support

The personnel available to operate this program is key to its quality. It seems essential that with a new enterprise of this type, having adequate time for planning, selection and training of staff, and collaboration with community partners is paramount. A patchwork of staff assigned extra duties will not work. It is planned that one full time person will direct the two proposed Learning Centers. The intent is to try and assure integrity in the management process of this project from the very beginning. The Project Director will be hired by the Bayfield School District and will be supported by a Management Council composed of designated representatives from each cooperating agency in the community. The function of this group is to guide implementation, provide continuous coordination and review of ongoing evaluation of the programs as the Learning Centers come into operation and move forward with their programs. This council has already operated for two years and is involved with communitywide planning and human resource services coordination. The membership includes tribal officials, county agency representatives, school and intermediate district staff and several elected officials including the mayor of Bayfield. Further, the project will operate along clear guidelines concerning nondiscrimination in hiring and all other aspects of program development and operation. Adherence to these guidelines and the use of procedures to assure their incorporation into decision making will produce equity and full participation by the entire range of students and parents in need. Of particular importance is the use of public informational meetings in community sites to give all interested parties an opportunity to become knowledgeable about program planning, possible employment opportunities and to develop an awareness about program services. Television coverage of Management Council meetings on the local cable service's public service coverage is being examined to help reach a wider audience in the community.

2) Assuring Diversity and a Community Voice

This project proposes to use a new activity as a major piece of the strategy to gain input and feedback from various individuals and organizations which have a stake in the community and the success of its members. *FAMILY COMMUNITY SUPPERS* will be held three times a year to celebrate accomplishments of the young people in the Bayfield area and promote community discussion on a topical issue. The meals will be free to all who wish to attend. The Suppers parallel a long established American Indian tradition of gathering for a "feast", a way to celebrate, to discuss, to share, to evaluate and to join together. This activity holds great promise for meeting the needs of this project and for building a consensus and involvement on the part of a wide range of community members. The Suppers will supplement the regular input and guidance available through monthly Management Council meetings. This group has agreed to be the ongoing oversight mechanism for the project.

The Management Council has a very broad membership including a number of tribal government representatives and students are also involved via Red Cliff Junior Tribal Council representatives. Specific processes and procedures planned for assuring community opinion is reflected in the Learning Center operations and are contained in the Iowa Safe Communities Program which will be adapted to our setting. The Safe Communities Program was designed to provide an integrated assessment, planning and programming concerning the issue of alcohol and drug abuse. Developed in part through a federal Community Activity Block Grant, Project SAFE "is to facilitate the education and involvement of every sector of communities so that community systems can take responsibility for reducing the incidence of alcohol and other drug use/abuse and associated problems. In the process, important steps will be taken that build healthy communities." The project outlines an organizational design quite similar to the Resilient Learner model adopted for the Learning Centers. Project SAFE is seen as a very effective tool to use in final project planning and helping to determine ongoing program activities. It is the structure through which the Family and Community Connections portion of the Resilient Learner model will be implemented.

- PROJECT EVALUATION -

Evaluation of the project will involve assessing the two main facets of the Learning Centers' programs; student attainment and satisfaction of parent/community objectives. First, the program's impact on student performance will be assessed through the examination of portfolio contents of the participating students. Portfolio assessment is selected because it has proven quite valuable since it involves the students in establishing goals and objectives for themselves and crinkling their progress toward those goals. The importance to a person of establishing goals for achievement is widely appreciated in both educational and business settings. This requires more work than more customary models of testing to determine attainment, but has the advantages of actively involving the learner and is a skill which can be applied by the student to a variety of life situations. That is not to say that some more conventional measures of student progress will be ignored. Such data as attendance, meeting deadlines, grades in daily class assignments, or test scores will not be ignored. These data will be incorporated into the portfolio as relatively objective measures which students and Learning Center leaders can include in the portfolio as measures whereby students can gauge their progress toward attaining stated goals and objectives which they have selected. A second benefit of this strategy for evaluation is that it prepares students for a kind of self analysis and information gathering that is particularly suited to career orientation and preparation of a resume for employment in the future. A third benefit of portfolios is that their use is very responsive to the relatively individualized nature of the proposed after-school program which will reflect a rather high degree of diversity in activities and degrees of involvement by various participants. The school district has some experience with this method of evaluation and is moving toward adopting this strategy on a whole school basis. The district's use of portfolios for students is facilitated at Bayfield by the University of Wisconsin–Stout through their Project Talent Program and the Cooperative Educational Service Area No. 12 (CESA No. 12) through its Northwest Regional Career Center. Periodic review of these portfolios will be completed by students with their tutors so that summary descriptive data are available to gauge progress of both individual students and to guide program development.

Satisfaction of parent/community objectives will also be assessed through the use of portfolios. Each tutor, each community partner representative and each volunteer will manage their own portfolio as a tool with which to gauge attainment of program goals and agency objectives and guide ongoing service delivery to the program, its students and families. It is planned that leadership portfolios will use computer and other technology to expedite recording of data and summarizing that information for use by the Learning Centers Director, school officials and the participating agencies. This is possible because the community currently has a modest computer network with workstations free to all citizens located at public libraries and educational centers in Red Cliff, Madeline Island, and Bayfield. The district offers basic computer training to all members of the community at all three locations. This project will significantly enhance this investment. It is expected that the computer network, through its connection to the internet's World Wide Web, will become an additional avenue by which all community members can monitor the progress of the project and provide comment about the program's impact upon the community. Creation and maintenance of Web pages for information and feedback is a goal for students who are eager to have a meaningful project through which to hone their emerging computer literacy.

This strategy calls for all members of the project to be involved with evaluation; leadership and participants alike. It will provide role modeling by adults as they complete their portfolios which students can imitate. The process will give the student and parent participants an important measure of control over their involvement and its outcomes. Each person will have a tangible product that they have created in the process of learning. This process will also provide the data needed by leadership to assess the ongoing success of various project elements and adjust those as the program matures.

6 | Why Some Proposals Fail

There are any number of reasons why many proposals for federal and private sector funding fail to result in a grant. Some of the reasons have to do with the way a grant proposal is written; others focus on concerns the grant awarding agency may have about your organization's abilities. Additionally, proposals may be rejected because they do not match the funding source's eligibility requirements or program priorities.

Common Weaknesses of Grant Proposals

First, let's look at what a number of grant awarding agencies and organizations consider some of the most common weaknesses of grant proposals.

> **Non-responsiveness to the grantmaker's requests.** The failure to respond to specific requests for information about such things as staffing, organization qualifications and technical capabilities is one of the most common reasons proposals do not get funded. Be certain that you demonstrate a full understanding of the problem being addressed in the request for proposals (RFP), offer a program that addresses the stated requirements and provide all of the requested information. Also, taking issue with an RFP directive may result in disqualification for non-responsiveness.

> **Use of the funding source's language to describe the problem, needs or work effort.** Repeating the language contained in an RFP to describe the problem, needs, work effort, or other requirements does not effectively demonstrate that you understand the purpose of the grant program for which you are applying.

> **Use of pompous words and phrases which convey no meaning.** Many funding sources reject proposals that are not written in plain English because they do not clearly explain the goals of your proposal. In addition, do not use jargon. You must remember that the person who is reading your proposal may not be an expert in your field and will not understand current "buzz words" or jargon.

> **Use of claims instead of facts.** Funding sources, when reviewing grant proposals, look for hard facts presented in a clear, easy-to-read format. Avoid the overuse of superlatives.

> **Excessive use of footnotes and references to "prove your point."** By writing a proposal in this way, funding sources develop a feeling that your proposal lacks self-confidence and contains no original thinking.

> **Use of vague generalizations and promises.** This weakness often results in a rambling proposal devoid of a well-thought-out plan of action.

> **Offering a weak or non-existent management plan.** You must provide clear evidence of being able to manage the proposed project if you expect any funding source to give you a large sum of money.

> **Failure to establish a direct line of communication.** There must be a direct line of communication between the funding source's project manager and your project manager. No funding source wishes to go through a bureaucracy, committee

or low-level manager to receive information about the project in which it has invested money.

➤ **Making unwarranted assumptions.** Occasionally assumptions must be made, but always know when you are working on an assumption. For example, in the absence of clear instructions, instead of assuming that quarterly progress reports will be required, indicate that progress reports will be quarterly unless more frequent reports are desired by the funding source.

➤ **Overuse of "boilerplate" material.** Boilerplate – or standard – material left over from prior proposal efforts is often used to produce quick and dirty proposals in the hope of getting lucky. Rather than assembling proposals from remnants of earlier efforts, take the time to write a good thoughtful presentation.

➤ **Writing the proposal before all the research is completed.** Before you start writing, do your homework by gathering and organizing all the information you will need. For example, pull together a list of your board of directors, your staff's resumes, proof of nonprofit status, if applicable, and your organization's financial records. You will also want to double-check to make sure that the funder to whom you plan to submit the proposal funds your type of organization or project and is accepting applications. This extra planning and effort will assist in your thinking and writing process.

Now that you have a better understanding of some of the most commonly seen weaknesses of grant proposals, let's take a look at some other concerns funding sources typically have. In particular, let's take a look at the management concerns many funding sources have cited as reasons for rejecting grant proposals.

Funding sources need solid, convincing evidence that the proposed project will be managed effectively. They need the details of internal control that go beyond standard general assurances of "good project management." Offer solid evidence that you (and your organization) understand what needs to be done to provide good management and that you have all the tools required (e.g. policies, plans, procedures, forms and documentation).

Addressing Common Concerns About Project Management

Here are some typical questions funding sources ask about the ability of an organization to successfully manage a funded project.

➤ Is the organization structured especially to meet the needs of the proposed project? In your proposal, you must show that your organization is set up in a way that is functional and is able to carry out the project.

➤ Has the project manager been given enough authority (or does he or she have inherent authority) to make key decisions and direct the funder's resources to support the project as necessary? If a potential funder asks about an organization's "lines of communication," the funder is really looking for the lines of authority under which your organization operates, and exactly where in that line of authority the manager for the funded project ranks.

➤ Is the location of the project office satisfactory? The funding source may look with favor on a project office location that is in close proximity to its own office.

➤ Does the organization show evidence of its ability to react swiftly to changing conditions? The funding source may expect a quick reaction to at least some critical events as they unfold and wants assurances that your organization can respond accordingly.

➤ Has the organization identified the proper milestones and objectives of each task? Most projects must be broken down into tasks which can then be assigned and monitored throughout their duration.

➤ Has the organization provided detailed expectations, including responsibilities and duties, of how each staff member will function? This is a key element of the proposal review process because a funding source wants clear and convincing evidence that your entire organization is prepared to carry out the proposed project; not just a few key players.

➤ Has the organization demonstrated controls and procedures for handling contingencies, ensuring schedule adherence and maintaining a high-quality product? In other words, make sure that your organization has shown in its proposal that it is prepared to handle the project for which you are seeking funds.

➤ Does the project manager have the ability to add and reduce staff rapidly, as required? Most funding sources are concerned about the peaks and valleys of activity during a project and want assurances that staff time and money will not be wasted.

➤ Has the organization shown clear plans to meet contingencies using alternative resources and plans to use them in the event a planned activity fails to produce or materialize? The funding source wants to be assured that your organization has back-up plans in place so that the proposed project will be carried out even if unforeseen problems arise.

➤ Has the organization presented evidence of cost-consciousness and procedures for cost control? The funding source wants to see proof that your organization is fiscally responsible and that you will not frivolously spend its money.

The Unpredictable Element: Human Nature

Aside from the common weaknesses of grant proposals and the management concerns most often expressed by funding sources, there is another element that must be considered: human nature.

Before writing your proposal, consider these points of view:

➤ **People tend to believe what they want to believe.** If the reviewer of your proposal rejects what you have written as unbelievable, too difficult to grasp or contrary to what he or she already believes, your proposal has failed.

➤ **Logic cannot overcome bias.** Beginning sentences with "Clearly" and "It is obvious that ..." is unlikely to overcome a strong bias that is already present. In fact, the use of such phrases may be counterproductive by calling attention to a weak argument.

➤ **The validity of any argument depends on the acceptance of the stated premises.** Your proposal reviewer may reject your premises because he or she knows them to be false, or is biased against them. Since you cannot compel the reviewer to accept your premises, you must look for sympathetic funding sources and attempt to persuade through a combination of logic, clarity of message, accuracy and organization.

It is important that you take these points of view into account when writing your proposal. While it is not always possible to change a reviewer's opinions, you can attempt to influence the reviewer's perception of your organization and proposed project.

When writing your proposal:

➤ Take into consideration any of the reviewer's known biases and present a convincing argument that makes the reviewer reconsider those biases.

➤ Gauge what your reviewer wants to see in the proposal, whether conscious or unconscious, and provide it.

➤ Be sure of your facts, when you offer facts. Proven facts can weaken any bias, no matter how strongly held. But if you are unsure of the facts you are presenting, leave them out. Unproven statements presented as fact only give the reviewer more reason to believe his or her bias.

➤ Avoid emotion–laden words which are likely to catalyze reviewer biases.

➤ Be sure your arguments are logically sound. Even though logic rarely overcomes a bias, presenting illogical information only serves to reinforce it.

⑦ Forms to Use When Seeking Grant Funds

Whether you are applying for a grant from a corporate giver, a private or public foundation or a federal agency, at some point in time you will have to fill out standard forms that provide information about your organization and staff, the proposed project, the budget and your plans for management and evaluation. It is extremely rare for a funder to award grant funds simply on the basis of a cover letter and a project narrative.

The basics of good grantsmanship discussed in Chapter 3 apply when completing these forms. Be sure to write concisely, fill in all the information requested as completely and accurately as possible, follow any and all instructions and have someone proofread your forms. Remember to include a cover letter, sign your form and type all of the information in the space provided. It is extremely important that you do not exceed page counts or space limitations since doing so raises questions about your ability to follow instructions.

In this chapter you will find reprints of many of the standard forms that must be submitted with your federal or private grant proposal.

Standard Federal Forms

There are several standard forms that must be included in any grant application submitted to a federal agency. However, keep in mind that most programs will ask for additional information and forms, such as a project summary and, if applicable, proof of your organization's nonprofit status as evidenced by your Internal Revenue Service determination letter.

The following are the federal grant application forms reproduced in this chapter:
Standard Form 424, Application for Federal Assistance
Standard Form 424A, Budget Information – Non–Construction Programs
Standard Form 424B, Assurances – Non–Construction Programs
Standard Form 424C, Budget Information – Construction Programs
Standard Form 424D, Assurances – Construction Programs
Standard Form LLL, Disclosure of Lobbying Activities
Certification Regarding Debarment, Suspension, Ineligibility and Voluntary Exclusion –
    Lower Tier Covered Transactions

Always check with the federal grantmaking agency and use the forms provided by the agency when you are requesting support from the federal government.

Common Grant Application Forms for Foundations

To make the grantseeking process easier and more efficient, many regional foundations and corporations have united to develop what they call "common grant application forms." Any organization that is a member of a regional grantmakers association will accept the association's common grant application forms.

To give you an idea of the information that will be requested and the format you will likely be asked to use, a sample of a common grant application form of the Minnesota Council on Foundations is provided. Included in the sample Foundation Common Grant Application Form is a cover sheet, proposal narrative and budget.

Again, you must remember that each grantmaker is different and will have different guidelines, program requirements, deadlines and priorities. Further, most grantmakers will ask you for additional information, such as a list of your board of directors, a project narrative, letters of commitment and support, and similar supporting evidence. You must do your homework.

Call or write to the foundation to which you are interested in submitting an application to request copies of any giving guidelines. Always contact the potential funder before submitting a common grant application form. Not all foundations use the common grant application form.

The common grant application forms included here are an example of one regional association's materials. Forms do vary from region to region, and in some cases, there may not be a common grant application form. To find out if the grantmaker you are interested in accepts one of the regional common grant application forms, check first with the funder's grantmaking officials. In addition, the Foundation Center maintains a database of regional grantmaking associations, along with links to the common grant application forms of each association. Contact the Foundation Center at (212) 620-4230, or visit the Web site at **http://www.foundationcenter.org.**

Electronic Applications

You should also note that with the recent advances in technology, a handful of grantmakers – in both the private and public sectors – are starting to convert to electronic or online grants processes.

Many of the telecommunications industry's corporate giving programs, for example, have established a process that will allow you to submit a letter of inquiry and, often, even a full proposal online. You simply have to access the grantmaker's Web site and follow the instructions and links provided.

The federal government is also testing the waters of online grantmaking. The National Science Foundation's FastLane, for example, allows users to submit their entire proposal via the Internet and also allows online grant award administration. The entire grantseeking and awards process is virtually paperless.

In some instances, a grantmaker will require you to submit your proposal in an electronic format. However, in most instances, grantmakers who have electronic application procedures will offer you the choice between an electronic submission and a traditional written proposal. Each grantmaker's proposal submission requirements will be specified in its giving guidelines or in the request for proposals that it issues.

*Editor's Note: This common grant application form was reprinted with permission from the Minnesota Council on Foundations. For more information on the council or on Minnesota grantmaking, call the council at (612) 338-1989; on the Web, **http://www.mcf.org**.*

Minnesota Common Grant Application Form

COVER SHEET   Date of Application:_____

(You may reproduce this form on your computer)

ORGANIZATION INFORMATION

_____
Legal Name of Organization

_____
Address

_____
City, State, Zip   Telephone   FAX

Individuals Responsible:

_____
Name of top paid staff   Title   Direct Dial Phone #

_____
Contact person (if different from top paid staff)   Title   Direct Dial Phone #

Organization Description: (2-3 sentences)

Is your organization an IRS 501(c)(3) not-for-profit?   _____YES   _____NO
   If no, is your organization a public agency/unit
   of government or religious institution: _____YES   _____NO

   If no, name of fiscal agent (fiscal sponsor): _____

AMOUNT AND TYPE OF SUPPORT REQUESTED

The dollar amount being requested: $_____

Funds are being requested for (make sure the funder provides the type of support you are requesting, then check the appropriate line):
_____ general operating support   _____ capital   _____ Other: _____
_____ project support   _____ endowment
_____ start-up costs   _____ technical assistance

If a project, give project duration   _____ Month _____Year   to   _____Month _____Year
If operating support, fiscal year: _____ Month _____Year   to   _____Month _____Year

BUDGET

Total annual organization budget: $_____

Total project budget (for support other than general operating): $_____

PROPOSAL SUMMARY

(If operating or start-up support, relate to the organization. If project and other support, relate to the project.)

Project name (if applying for project support): _____
Please give a 2-3 sentence summary of the request:

Geographic area served:

Population served:

AUTHORIZATION

Name of top paid staff and/or Board Chair (type):   _____

Signature: _____

Minnesota Common Grant Application Form (continued)

Proposal Narrative

Please provide the following information in narrative form in this order. Five to seven pages or less is recommended excluding attachments. (Be sure to include a cover letter which introduces your organization and proposal and makes a strategic link between your proposal and the mission and grantmaking interest of each funder to whom you apply.)

A. ORGANIZATIONAL INFORMATION

1. Brief summary of organization history.
2. Brief summary of organization mission and goals.
3. Description of current programs, activities, service statistics, and strengths/accomplishments.
4. Your organization's relationship with other organizations working to meet the same needs or providing similar services. Please explain how you differ from these other agencies.
5. Number of board members, full time paid staff, part-time paid staff, and volunteers.

B. PURPOSE OF GRANT

1. Situation
   - The *situation*—opportunity, problem, issue, need, and the community—that your proposal addresses.
   - *How* that focus was determined.
   - *Who* was involved in that decision-making process.

2. Specific activities
   - *Specific activities* for which you seek funding.
   - *Who* will carry out those activities. (If individuals are known, describe qualifications.)
   - Your overall goal(s).
   - Specific objectives or ways in which you will meet the goal(s).
   - Actions that will accomplish your objectives.
   - Time frame in which all this will take place.

3. Impact of activities
   - How the proposed activities will benefit the community in which they will occur, being as clear as you can about the *impact* you expect to have.
   - Long-term strategies (if applicable) for sustaining this effort.

C. EVALUATION

1. How will you measure the effectiveness of your activities.
2. Your criteria (measurable, if possible) for a successful program and the results you expect to have achieved by the end of the funding period.
3. Who will be involved in evaluating this work (staff, board, constituents, community, consultants).
4. How will evaluations be used.

ATTACHMENTS

Be sure to check each funders guidelines. Generally the following is required

1. Finances
   - Financial statements from your most recently completed fiscal year, whether audited or unaudited.
   - Organization and/or Project Budget (see attached form).
   - List names of corporations and foundations that you are soliciting for funding, with dollar amounts, indicating which sources are committed, pending, or anticipated.

2. Other Supporting Materials
   - List of board members and their affiliations.
   - One-paragraph description of key staff, including qualifications relevant to the specific request.
   - A copy of your current IRS determination letter (or your fiscal agent's) indicating tax-exempt status.

Minnesota Common Grant Application Form (continued)

BUDGET

(You may reporduce this form on your computer)

If you already prepare organization and project budgets that contain this information, please feel free to submit them in their original forms. For project proposals, most grantmakers will request both organization and project budgets.

Check which budget(s) are included: _____ Organization Budget _____ Project Budget

Budget for the period: _____ to _____

INCOME		EXPENSE		
Source	Amount	Item	Amount	% FT/PT
Support				
Government grants & contracts	$	Salaries & wages (for project budgets breakdown by individual position and indicate full or part time.)	$	
Foundations	$		$	
Corporations	$		$	
United Way or other federated campaigns	$		$	
Individual contributions	$		$	
Fundraising events & products	$	Subtotal	$	%
Membership income	$	Insurance benefits & other related taxes	$	
In-kind support	$	Consultants & professional fees	$	
		Travel	$	
Revenue				
Earned Income	$	Equipment	$	
Other (specify)	$	Supplies	$	
	$	Printing & copying	$	
	$	Telephone & fax	$	
	$	Postage & delivery	$	
	$	Rent & utilities	$	
	$	In-kind expenses	$	
	$	Other (specify)	$	
	$		$	
Total Income:	$	**Total Expense:**	$	
		Difference (income less expense)	$	

Grantmakers That Accept The Minnesota Common Grant Application Form

The following funders have agreed to accept the Minnesota Common Grant Application Form. Before sending an application to any of the funders listed, be sure to contact them directly for their specific requirements.

Some of the funders below may require a letter of inquiry or additional or supplementary information. They are noted with double asterisk (**). You must contact these funders directly to find out what they need in addition to this form.

American Express Financial Advisors, Inc.**
Hugh J. Andersen Foundation**
Baker Foundation
Lillian Wright & C. Emil Berglund Foundation
Best Buy Company, Inc.
Blandin Foundation**
Bloomington Community Foundation**
Blue Cross and Blue Shield of Minnesota Foundation**
Otto Bremer Foundation**
The Cargill Foundation**
Carolyn Foundation**
Central Minnesota Community Foundation
Charlson Research Foundation**
Albert W. Cherne Foundation**
Dain Bosworth Foundation**
Dayton Hudson Foundation**
The Donaldson Foundation
Duluth–Superior Area Community Foundation**
The Jaye F. and Betty F. Dyer Foundation
Edwards Memorial Trust
Fargo–Moorhead Area Foundation**
H. B. Fuller Company Foundation
General Mills Foundation**
The Graco Foundation**
Grotto Foundation
Honeywell Foundation
HRK Foundation**
Initiative Foundation**
International Multifoods Foundation**
The Jostens Foundation**
Marbrook Foundation

The Medtronic Foundation
The Minneapolis Foundation**
Minnesota Mutual Foundation
M-O-M Cares Employee Foundation
Northern States Power Company**
Northland Foundation**
Northwest Minnesota Foundation**
Norwest Foundation**
Onan Family Foundation**
Ordean Foundation**
Pentair Foundation**
Perkins Foundation**
Philanthrofund Foundation**
The Elizabeth C. Quinlan Foundation, Inc.
The Rathmann Family Foundation**
Reliant Energy Minnesota
ReliaStar Foundation**
Ripley Memorial Foundation**
Rochester Area Foundation
Saunders Family Foundation
R.C. Skoe Foundation
The St. Paul Companies**
Star Tribune Foundation
TCF Foundation
James R. Thorpe Foundation**
U.S. Bancorp Foundation**
DeWitt & Caroline Van Evera Foundation**
Archie D. and Bertha H. Walker Foundation**
The Wasie Foundation**
WCA Foundation**
Wendel Foundation**
West Central Initiative**
Williams Steel & Hardware

This list is current as of March 1, 1997. If a grantmaker is not listed above, be sure to ask if they accept the Minnesota Common Grant Application Form when you request guidelines.

Standard Form 424

APPLICATION FOR FEDERAL ASSISTANCE

OMB Approval No. 0348-0043

2. DATE SUBMITTED	Applicant Identifier

1. TYPE OF SUBMISSION:		3. DATE RECEIVED BY STATE	State Application Identifier
Application	Preapplication		
☐ Construction	☐ Construction	4. DATE RECEIVED BY FEDERAL AGENCY	Federal Identifier
☐ Non-Construction	☐ Non-Construction		

5. APPLICANT INFORMATION

Legal Name:	Organizational Unit:
Address (give city, county, State, and zip code):	Name and telephone number of person to be contacted on matters involving this application (give area code)

6. EMPLOYER IDENTIFICATION NUMBER (EIN):

☐☐ – ☐☐☐☐☐☐☐

7. TYPE OF APPLICANT: (enter appropriate letter in box) ☐

A. State   H. Independent School Dist.
B. County   I. State Controlled Institution of Higher Learning
C. Municipal   J. Private University
D. Township   K. Indian Tribe
E. Interstate   L. Individual
F. Intermunicipal   M. Profit Organization
G. Special District   N. Other (Specify) _____

8. TYPE OF APPLICATION:

☐ New   ☐ Continuation   ☐ Revision

If Revision, enter appropriate letter(s) in box(es)   ☐ ☐

A. Increase Award   B. Decrease Award   C. Increase Duration
D. Decrease Duration   Other(specify):

9. NAME OF FEDERAL AGENCY:

10. CATALOG OF FEDERAL DOMESTIC ASSISTANCE NUMBER:

☐☐ – ☐☐☐

TITLE:

11. DESCRIPTIVE TITLE OF APPLICANT'S PROJECT:

12. AREAS AFFECTED BY PROJECT (Cities, Counties, States, etc.):

13. PROPOSED PROJECT		**14. CONGRESSIONAL DISTRICTS OF:**	
Start Date	Ending Date	a. Applicant	b. Project

15. ESTIMATED FUNDING:

a. Federal	$	.00
b. Applicant	$	.00
c. State	$	.00
d. Local	$	.00
e. Other	$	.00
f. Program Income	$	.00
g. TOTAL	$	.00

16. IS APPLICATION SUBJECT TO REVIEW BY STATE EXECUTIVE ORDER 12372 PROCESS?

a. YES. THIS PREAPPLICATION/APPLICATION WAS MADE AVAILABLE TO THE STATE EXECUTIVE ORDER 12372 PROCESS FOR REVIEW ON:

DATE _____

b. No. ☐ PROGRAM IS NOT COVERED BY E. O. 12372
☐ OR PROGRAM HAS NOT BEEN SELECTED BY STATE FOR REVIEW

17. IS THE APPLICANT DELINQUENT ON ANY FEDERAL DEBT?

☐ Yes   If "Yes," attach an explanation.   ☐ No

18. TO THE BEST OF MY KNOWLEDGE AND BELIEF, ALL DATA IN THIS APPLICATION/PREAPPLICATION ARE TRUE AND CORRECT, THE DOCUMENT HAS BEEN DULY AUTHORIZED BY THE GOVERNING BODY OF THE APPLICANT AND THE APPLICANT WILL COMPLY WITH THE ATTACHED ASSURANCES IF THE ASSISTANCE IS AWARDED.

a. Type Name of Authorized Representative	b. Title	c. Telephone Number
d. Signature of Authorized Representative		e. Date Signed

Previous Edition Usable
Authorized for Local Reproduction

Standard Form 424 (Rev. 7-97)
Prescribed by OMB Circular A-102

INSTRUCTIONS FOR THE SF-424

Public reporting burden for this collection of information is estimated to average 45 minutes per response, including time for reviewing instructions, searching existing data sources, gathering and maintaining the data needed, and completing and reviewing the collection of information. Send comments regarding the burden estimate or any other aspect of this collection of information, including suggestions for reducing this burden, to the Office of Management and Budget, Paperwork Reduction Project (0348-0043), Washington, DC 20503.

PLEASE DO NOT RETURN YOUR COMPLETED FORM TO THE OFFICE OF MANAGEMENT AND BUDGET. SEND IT TO THE ADDRESS PROVIDED BY THE SPONSORING AGENCY.

This is a standard form used by applicants as a required facesheet for preapplications and applications submitted for Federal assistance. It will be used by Federal agencies to obtain applicant certification that States which have established a review and comment procedure in response to Executive Order 12372 and have selected the program to be included in their process, have been given an opportunity to review the applicant's submission.

Item: Entry:

1. Self-explanatory.

2. Date application submitted to Federal agency (or State if applicable) and applicant's control number (if applicable).

3. State use only (if applicable).

4. If this application is to continue or revise an existing award, enter present Federal identifier number. If for a new project, leave blank.

5. Legal name of applicant, name of primary organizational unit which will undertake the assistance activity, complete address of the applicant, and name and telephone number of the person to contact on matters related to this application.

6. Enter Employer Identification Number (EIN) as assigned by the Internal Revenue Service.

7. Enter the appropriate letter in the space provided.

8. Check appropriate box and enter appropriate letter(s) in the space(s) provided:

    -- "New" means a new assistance award.

    -- "Continuation" means an extension for an additional funding/budget period for a project with a projected completion date.

    -- "Revision" means any change in the Federal Government's financial obligation or contingent liability from an existing obligation.

9. Name of Federal agency from which assistance is being requested with this application.

10. Use the Catalog of Federal Domestic Assistance number and title of the program under which assistance is requested.

11. Enter a brief descriptive title of the project. If more than one program is involved, you should append an explanation on a separate sheet. If appropriate (e.g., construction or real property projects), attach a map showing project location. For preapplications, use a separate sheet to provide a summary description of this project.

Item: Entry:

12. List only the largest political entities affected (e.g., State, counties, cities).

13. Self-explanatory.

14. List the applicant's Congressional District and any District(s) affected by the program or project.

15. Amount requested or to be contributed during the first funding/budget period by each contributor. Value of in-kind contributions should be included on appropriate lines as applicable. If the action will result in a dollar change to an existing award, indicate _only_ the amount of the change. For decreases, enclose the amounts in parentheses. If both basic and supplemental amounts are included, show breakdown on an attached sheet. For multiple program funding, use totals and show breakdown using same categories as item 15.

16. Applicants should contact the State Single Point of Contact (SPOC) for Federal Executive Order 12372 to determine whether the application is subject to the State intergovernmental review process.

17. This question applies to the applicant organization, not the person who signs as the authorized representative. Categories of debt include delinquent audit disallowances, loans and taxes.

18. To be signed by the authorized representative of the applicant. A copy of the governing body's authorization for you to sign this application as official representative must be on file in the applicant's office. (Certain Federal agencies may require that this authorization be submitted as part of the application.)

SF-424 (Rev. 7-97) Back

Standard Form 424A

OMB Approval No. 0348-0044

BUDGET INFORMATION - Non-Construction Programs

SECTION A - BUDGET SUMMARY

Grant Program Function or Activity (a)	Catalog of Federal Domestic Assistance Number (b)	Estimated Unobligated Funds		New or Revised Budget		
		Federal (c)	Non-Federal (d)	Federal (e)	Non-Federal (f)	Total (g)
1.		$				$
2.						
3.						
4.						
5. Totals		$				$

SECTION B - BUDGET CATEGORIES

6. Object Class Categories	GRANT PROGRAM, FUNCTION OR ACTIVITY				Total
	(1)	(2)	(3)	(4)	(5)
a. Personnel	$	$	$	$	$
b. Fringe Benefits					
c. Travel					
d. Equipment					
e. Supplies					
f. Contractual					
g. Construction					
h. Other					
i. Total Direct Charges (sum of 6a-6h)					
j. Indirect Charges					
k. TOTALS (sum of 6i and 6j)	$	$	$	$	$
7. Program Income	$	$	$	$	$

Authorized for Local Reproduction

Standard Form 424A (Rev. 7-97)
Prescribed by OMB Circular A-102

SECTION C - NON-FEDERAL RESOURCES

	(a) Grant Program	(b) Applicant	(c) State	(d) Other Sources	(e) TOTALS
8.		$	$		$
9.					
10.					
11.					
12. TOTAL (sum of lines 8-11)		$	$	$	$

SECTION D - FORECASTED CASH NEEDS

	Total for 1st Year	1st Quarter	2nd Quarter	3rd Quarter	4th Quarter
13. Federal	$	$	$	$	$
14. Non-Federal					
15. TOTAL (sum of lines 13 and 14)	$	$	$	$	$

SECTION E - BUDGET ESTIMATES OF FEDERAL FUNDS NEEDED FOR BALANCE OF THE PROJECT

	(a) Grant Program	FUTURE FUNDING PERIODS (Years)			
		(b) First	(c) Second	(d) Third	(e) Fourth
16.		$	$	$	$
17.					
18.					
19.					
20. TOTAL (sum of lines 16-19)		$	$	$	$

SECTION F - OTHER BUDGET INFORMATION

21. Direct Charges:

22. Indirect Charges:

23. Remarks:

INSTRUCTIONS FOR THE SF-424A

Public reporting burden for this collection of information is estimated to average 180 minutes per response, including time for reviewing instructions, searching existing data sources, gathering and maintaining the data needed, and completing and reviewing the collection of information. Send comments regarding the burden estimate or any other aspect of this collection of information, including suggestions for reducing this burden, to the Office of Management and Budget, Paperwork Reduction Project (0348-0044), Washington, DC 20503.

PLEASE DO NOT RETURN YOUR COMPLETED FORM TO THE OFFICE OF MANAGEMENT AND BUDGET. SEND IT TO THE ADDRESS PROVIDED BY THE SPONSORING AGENCY.

General Instructions

This form is designed so that application can be made for funds from one or more grant programs. In preparing the budget, adhere to any existing Federal grantor agency guidelines which prescribe how and whether budgeted amounts should be separately shown for different functions or activities within the program. For some programs, grantor agencies may require budgets to be separately shown by function or activity. For other programs, grantor agencies may require a breakdown by function or activity. Sections A, B, C, and D should include budget estimates for the whole project except when applying for assistance which requires Federal authorization in annual or other funding period increments. In the latter case, Sections A, B, C, and D should provide the budget for the first budget period (usually a year) and Section E should present the need for Federal assistance in the subsequent budget periods. All applications should contain a breakdown by the object class categories shown in Lines a-k of Section B.

Section A. Budget Summary Lines 1-4 Columns (a) and (b)

For applications pertaining to a *single* Federal grant program (Federal Domestic Assistance Catalog number) and *not requiring* a functional or activity breakdown, enter on Line 1 under Column (a) the Catalog program title and the Catalog number in Column (b).

For applications pertaining to a *single* program *requiring* budget amounts by multiple functions or activities, enter the name of each activity or function on each line in Column (a), and enter the Catalog number in Column (b). For applications pertaining to multiple programs where none of the programs require a breakdown by function or activity, enter the Catalog program title on each line in *Column* (a) and the respective Catalog number on each line in Column (b).

For applications pertaining to *multiple* programs where one or more programs *require* a breakdown by function or activity, prepare a separate sheet for each program requiring the breakdown. Additional sheets should be used when one form does not provide adequate space for all breakdown of data required. However, when more than one sheet is used, the first page should provide the summary totals by programs.

Lines 1-4, Columns (c) through (g)

For new applications, leave Column (c) and (d) blank. For each line entry in Columns (a) and (b), enter in Columns (e), (f), and (g) the appropriate amounts of funds needed to support the project for the first funding period (usually a year).

For continuing grant program applications, submit these forms before the end of each funding period as required by the grantor agency. Enter in Columns (c) and (d) the estimated amounts of funds which will remain unobligated at the end of the grant funding period only if the Federal grantor agency instructions provide for this. Otherwise, leave these columns blank. Enter in columns (e) and (f) the amounts of funds needed for the upcoming period. The amount(s) in Column (g) should be the sum of amounts in Columns (e) and (f).

For supplemental grants and changes to existing grants, do not use Columns (c) and (d). Enter in Column (e) the amount of the increase or decrease of Federal funds and enter in Column (f) the amount of the increase or decrease of non-Federal funds. In Column (g) enter the new total budgeted amount (Federal and non-Federal) which includes the total previous authorized budgeted amounts plus or minus, as appropriate, the amounts shown in Columns (e) and (f). The amount(s) in Column (g) should not equal the sum of amounts in Columns (e) and (f).

Line 5 - Show the totals for all columns used.

Section B Budget Categories

In the column headings (1) through (4), enter the titles of the same programs, functions, and activities shown on Lines 1-4, Column (a), Section A. When additional sheets are prepared for Section A, provide similar column headings on each sheet. For each program, function or activity, fill in the total requirements for funds (both Federal and non-Federal) by object class categories.

Line 6a-i - Show the totals of Lines 6a to 6h in each column.

Line 6j - Show the amount of indirect cost.

Line 6k - Enter the total of amounts on Lines 6i and 6j. For all applications for new grants and continuation grants the total amount in column (5), Line 6k, should be the same as the total amount shown in Section A, Column (g), Line 5. For supplemental grants and changes to grants, the total amount of the increase or decrease as shown in Columns (1)-(4), Line 6k should be the same as the sum of the amounts in Section A, Columns (e) and (f) on Line 5.

Line 7 - Enter the estimated amount of income, if any, expected to be generated from this project. Do not add or subtract this amount from the total project amount, Show under the program

SF-424A (Rev. 7-97) Page 3

INSTRUCTIONS FOR THE SF-424A (continued)

narrative statement the nature and source of income. The estimated amount of program income may be considered by the Federal grantor agency in determining the total amount of the grant.

Section C. Non-Federal Resources

Lines 8-11 Enter amounts of non-Federal resources that will be used on the grant. If in-kind contributions are included, provide a brief explanation on a separate sheet.

Column (a) - Enter the program titles identical to Column (a), Section A. A breakdown by function or activity is not necessary.

Column (b) - Enter the contribution to be made by the applicant.

Column (c) - Enter the amount of the State's cash and in-kind contribution if the applicant is not a State or State agency. Applicants which are a State or State agencies should leave this column blank.

Column (d) - Enter the amount of cash and in-kind contributions to be made from all other sources.

Column (e) - Enter totals of Columns (b), (c), and (d).

Line 12 - Enter the total for each of Columns (b)-(e). The amount in Column (e) should be equal to the amount on Line 5, Column (f), Section A.

Section D. Forecasted Cash Needs

Line 13 - Enter the amount of cash needed by quarter from the grantor agency during the first year.

Line 14 - Enter the amount of cash from all other sources needed by quarter during the first year.

Line 15 - Enter the totals of amounts on Lines 13 and 14.

Section E. Budget Estimates of Federal Funds Needed for Balance of the Project

Lines 16-19 - Enter in Column (a) the same grant program titles shown in Column (a), Section A. A breakdown by function or activity is not necessary. For new applications and continuation grant applications, enter in the proper columns amounts of Federal funds which will be needed to complete the program or project over the succeeding funding periods (usually in years). This section need not be completed for revisions (amendments, changes, or supplements) to funds for the current year of existing grants.

If more than four lines are needed to list the program titles, submit additional schedules as necessary.

Line 20 - Enter the total for each of the Columns (b)-(e). When additional schedules are prepared for this Section, annotate accordingly and show the overall totals on this line.

Section F. Other Budget Information

Line 21 - Use this space to explain amounts for individual direct object class cost categories that may appear to be out of the ordinary or to explain the details as required by the Federal grantor agency.

Line 22 - Enter the type of indirect rate (provisional, predetermined, final or fixed) that will be in effect during the funding period, the estimated amount of the base to which the rate is applied, and the total indirect expense.

Line 23 - Provide any other explanations or comments deemed necessary.

Standard Form 424B

OMB Approval No. 0348-0040

ASSURANCES - NON-CONSTRUCTION PROGRAMS

Public reporting burden for this collection of information is estimated to average 15 minutes per response, including time for reviewing instructions, searching existing data sources, gathering and maintaining the data needed, and completing and reviewing the collection of information. Send comments regarding the burden estimate or any other aspect of this collection of information, including suggestions for reducing this burden, to the Office of Management and Budget, Paperwork Reduction Project (0348-0040), Washington, DC 20503.

PLEASE DO NOT RETURN YOUR COMPLETED FORM TO THE OFFICE OF MANAGEMENT AND BUDGET. SEND IT TO THE ADDRESS PROVIDED BY THE SPONSORING AGENCY.

NOTE: Certain of these assurances may not be applicable to your project or program. If you have questions, please contact the awarding agency. Further, certain Federal awarding agencies may require applicants to certify to additional assurances. If such is the case, you will be notified.

As the duly authorized representative of the applicant, I certify that the applicant:

1. Has the legal authority to apply for Federal assistance and the institutional, managerial and financial capability (including funds sufficient to pay the non-Federal share of project cost) to ensure proper planning, management and completion of the project described in this application.

2. Will give the awarding agency, the Comptroller General of the United States and, if appropriate, the State, through any authorized representative, access to and the right to examine all records, books, papers, or documents related to the award; and will establish a proper accounting system in accordance with generally accepted accounting standards or agency directives.

3. Will establish safeguards to prohibit employees from using their positions for a purpose that constitutes or presents the appearance of personal or organizational conflict of interest, or personal gain.

4. Will initiate and complete the work within the applicable time frame after receipt of approval of the awarding agency.

5. Will comply with the Intergovernmental Personnel Act of 1970 (42 U.S.C. §§4728-4763) relating to prescribed standards for merit systems for programs funded under one of the 19 statutes or regulations specified in Appendix A of OPM's Standards for a Merit System of Personnel Administration (5 C.F.R. 900, Subpart F).

6. Will comply with all Federal statutes relating to nondiscrimination. These include but are not limited to: (a) Title VI of the Civil Rights Act of 1964 (P.L. 88-352) which prohibits discrimination on the basis of race, color or national origin; (b) Title IX of the Education Amendments of 1972, as amended (20 U.S.C. §§1681-1683, and 1685-1686), which prohibits discrimination on the basis of sex; (c) Section 504 of the Rehabilitation Act of 1973, as amended (29 U.S.C. §794), which prohibits discrimination on the basis of handicaps; (d) the Age Discrimination Act of 1975, as amended (42 U.S.C. §§6101-6107), which prohibits discrimination on the basis of age; (e) the Drug Abuse Office and Treatment Act of 1972 (P.L. 92-255), as amended, relating to nondiscrimination on the basis of drug abuse; (f) the Comprehensive Alcohol Abuse and Alcoholism Prevention, Treatment and Rehabilitation Act of 1970 (P.L. 91-616), as amended, relating to nondiscrimination on the basis of alcohol abuse or alcoholism; (g) §§523 and 527 of the Public Health Service Act of 1912 (42 U.S.C. §§290 dd-3 and 290 ee 3), as amended, relating to confidentiality of alcohol and drug abuse patient records; (h) Title VIII of the Civil Rights Act of 1968 (42 U.S.C. §§3601 et seq.), as amended, relating to nondiscrimination in the sale, rental or financing of housing; (i) any other nondiscrimination provisions in the specific statute(s) under which application for Federal assistance is being made; and, (j) the requirements of any other nondiscrimination statute(s) which may apply to the application.

7. Will comply, or has already complied, with the requirements of Titles II and III of the Uniform Relocation Assistance and Real Property Acquisition Policies Act of 1970 (P.L. 91-646) which provide for fair and equitable treatment of persons displaced or whose property is acquired as a result of Federal or federally-assisted programs. These requirements apply to all interests in real property acquired for project purposes regardless of Federal participation in purchases.

8. Will comply, as applicable, with provisions of the Hatch Act (5 U.S.C. §§1501-1508 and 7324-7328) which limit the political activities of employees whose principal employment activities are funded in whole or in part with Federal funds.

Previous Edition Usable

Authorized for Local Reproduction

Standard Form 424B (Rev. 7-97)
Prescribed by OMB Circular A-102

9. Will comply, as applicable, with the provisions of the Davis-Bacon Act (40 U.S.C. §§276a to 276a-7), the Copeland Act (40 U.S.C. §276c and 18 U.S.C. §874), and the Contract Work Hours and Safety Standards Act (40 U.S.C. §§327-333), regarding labor standards for federally-assisted construction subagreements.

10. Will comply, if applicable, with flood insurance purchase requirements of Section 102(a) of the Flood Disaster Protection Act of 1973 (P.L. 93-234) which requires recipients in a special flood hazard area to participate in the program and to purchase flood insurance if the total cost of insurable construction and acquisition is $10,000 or more.

11. Will comply with environmental standards which may be prescribed pursuant to the following: (a) institution of environmental quality control measures under the National Environmental Policy Act of 1969 (P.L. 91-190) and Executive Order (EO) 11514; (b) notification of violating facilities pursuant to EO 11738; (c) protection of wetlands pursuant to EO 11990; (d) evaluation of flood hazards in floodplains in accordance with EO 11988; (e) assurance of project consistency with the approved State management program developed under the Coastal Zone Management Act of 1972 (16 U.S.C. §§1451 et seq.); (f) conformity of Federal actions to State (Clean Air) Implementation Plans under Section 176(c) of the Clean Air Act of 1955, as amended (42 U.S.C. §§7401 et seq.); (g) protection of underground sources of drinking water under the Safe Drinking Water Act of 1974, as amended (P.L. 93-523); and, (h) protection of endangered species under the Endangered Species Act of 1973, as amended (P.L. 93-205).

12. Will comply with the Wild and Scenic Rivers Act of 1968 (16 U.S.C. §§1271 et seq.) related to protecting components or potential components of the national wild and scenic rivers system.

13. Will assist the awarding agency in assuring compliance with Section 106 of the National Historic Preservation Act of 1966, as amended (16 U.S.C. §470), EO 11593 (identification and protection of historic properties), and the Archaeological and Historic Preservation Act of 1974 (16 U.S.C. §§469a-1 et seq.).

14. Will comply with P.L. 93-348 regarding the protection of human subjects involved in research, development, and related activities supported by this award of assistance.

15. Will comply with the Laboratory Animal Welfare Act of 1966 (P.L. 89-544, as amended, 7 U.S.C. §§2131 et seq.) pertaining to the care, handling, and treatment of warm blooded animals held for research, teaching, or other activities supported by this award of assistance.

16. Will comply with the Lead-Based Paint Poisoning Prevention Act (42 U.S.C. §§4801 et seq.) which prohibits the use of lead-based paint in construction or rehabilitation of residence structures.

17. Will cause to be performed the required financial and compliance audits in accordance with the Single Audit Act Amendments of 1996 and OMB Circular No. A-133, "Audits of States, Local Governments, and Non-Profit Organizations."

18. Will comply with all applicable requirements of all other Federal laws, executive orders, regulations, and policies governing this program.

SIGNATURE OF AUTHORIZED CERTIFYING OFFICIAL	TITLE
APPLICANT ORGANIZATION	DATE SUBMITTED

Standard Form 424B (Rev. 7-97) Back

Standard Form 424C

BUDGET INFORMATION - Construction Programs

OMB Approval No. 0348-0041

NOTE: Certain Federal assistance programs require additional computations to arrive at the Federal share of project costs eligible for participation. If such is the case, you will be notified.

COST CLASSIFICATION	a. Total Cost	b. Costs Not Allowable for Participation	c. Total Allowable Costs (Columns a-b)
1. Administrative and legal expenses	$ .00	$ .00	$ .00
2. Land, structures, rights-of-way, appraisals, etc.	$ .00	$ .00	$ .00
3. Relocation expenses and payments	$ .00	$ .00	$ .00
4. Architectural and engineering fees	$ .00	$ .00	$ .00
5. Other architectural and engineering fees	$ .00	$ .00	$ .00
6. Project inspection fees	$ .00	$ .00	$ .00
7. Site work	$ .00	$ .00	$ .00
8. Demolition and removal	$ .00	$ .00	$ .00
9. Construction	$ .00	$ .00	$ .00
10. Equipment	$ .00	$ .00	$ .00
11. Miscellaneous	$ .00	$ .00	$ .00
12. SUBTOTAL (sum of lines 1-11)	$ .00	$ .00	$ .00
13. Contingencies	$ .00	$ .00	$ .00
14. SUBTOTAL	$ .00	$ .00	$ .00
15. Project (program) income	$ .00	$ .00	$ .00
16. TOTAL PROJECT COSTS (subtract #15 from #14)	$ .00	$ .00	$ .00

FEDERAL FUNDING

17. Federal assistance requested, calculate as follows: (Consult Federal agency for Federal percentage share.) Enter the resulting Federal share.

Enter eligible costs from line 16c Multiply X _____% $ .00

Standard Form 424C (Rev. 7-97)
Prescribed by OMB Circular A-102

INSTRUCTIONS FOR THE SF-424C

Public reporting burden for this collection of information is estimated to average 180 minutes per response, including time for reviewing instructions, searching existing data sources, gathering and maintaining the data needed, and completing and reviewing the collection of information. Send comments regarding the burden estimate or any other aspect of this collection of information, including suggestions for reducing this burden, to the Office of Management and Budget, Paperwork Reduction Project (0348-0041), Washington, DC 20503.

PLEASE DO NOT RETURN YOUR COMPLETED FORM TO THE OFFICE OF MANAGEMENT AND BUDGET. SEND IT TO THE ADDRESS PROVIDED BY THE SPONSORING AGENCY.

This sheet is to be used for the following types of applications: (1) "New" (means a new [previously unfunded] assistance award); (2) "Continuation" (means funding in a succeeding budget period which stemmed from a prior agreement to fund); and (3) "Revised" (means any changes in the Federal Government's financial obligations or contingent liability from an existing obligation). If there is no change in the award amount, there is no need to complete this form. Certain Federal agencies may require only an explanatory letter to effect minor (no cost) changes. If you have questions, please contact the Federal agency.

Column a. - If this is an application for a "New" project, enter the total estimated cost of each of the items listed on lines 1 through 16 (as applicable) under "COST CLASSIFICATION."

If this application entails a change to an existing award, enter the eligible amounts *approved under the previous award* for the items under "COST CLASSIFICATION."

Column b. - If this is an application for a "New" project, enter that portion of the cost of each item in Column a. which is *not* allowable for Federal assistance. Contact the Federal agency for assistance in determining the allowability of specific costs.

If this application entails a change to an existing award, enter the adjustment [+ or (-)] to the previously approved costs (from column a.) reflected in this application.

Column. - This is the net of lines 1 through 16 in columns "a." and "b."

Line 1 - Enter estimated amounts needed to cover administrative expenses. Do not include costs which are related to the normal functions of government. Allowable legal costs are generally only those associated with the purchases of land which is allowable for Federal participation and certain services in support of construction of the project.

Line 2 - Enter estimated site and right(s)-of-way acquisition costs (this includes purchase, lease, and/or easements).

Line 3 - Enter estimated costs related to relocation advisory assistance, replacement housing, relocation payments to displaced persons and businesses, etc.

Line 4 - Enter estimated basic engineering fees related to construction (this includes start-up services and preparation of project performance work plan).

Line 5 - Enter estimated engineering costs, such as surveys, tests, soil borings, etc.

Line 6 - Enter estimated engineering inspection costs.

Line 7 - Enter estimated costs of site preparation and restoration which are not included in the basic construction contract.

Line 9 - Enter estimated cost of the construction contract.

Line 10 - Enter estimated cost of office, shop, laboratory, safety equipment, etc. to be used at the facility, if such costs are not included in the construction contract.

Line 11 - Enter estimated miscellaneous costs.

Line 12 - Total of items 1 through 11.

Line 13 - Enter estimated contingency costs. (Consult the Federal agency for the percentage of the estimated construction cost to use.)

Line 14 - Enter the total of lines 12 and 13.

Line 15 - Enter estimated program income to be earned during the grant period, e.g., salvaged materials, etc.

Line 16 - Subtract line 15 from line 14.

Line 17 - This block is for the computation of the Federal share. Multiply the total allowable project costs from line 16, column "c." by the Federal percentage share (this may be up to 100 percent; consult Federal agency for Federal percentage share) and enter the product on line 17.

SF-424C (Rev. 7-97) Back

Standard Form 424D

OMB Approval No. 0348-0042

ASSURANCES - CONSTRUCTION PROGRAMS

Public reporting burden for this collection of information is estimated to average 15 minutes per response, including time for reviewing instructions, searching existing data sources, gathering and maintaining the data needed, and completing and reviewing the collection of information. Send comments regarding the burden estimate or any other aspect of this collection of information, including suggestions for reducing this burden, to the Office of Management and Budget, Paperwork Reduction Project (0348-0042), Washington, DC 20503.

PLEASE <u>DO NOT</u> RETURN YOUR COMPLETED FORM TO THE OFFICE OF MANAGEMENT AND BUDGET. SEND IT TO THE ADDRESS PROVIDED BY THE SPONSORING AGENCY.

NOTE: Certain of these assurances may not be applicable to your project or program. If you have questions, please contact the Awarding Agency. Further, certain Federal assistance awarding agencies may require applicants to certify to additional assurances. If such is the case, you will be notified.

As the duly authorized representative of the applicant, I certify that the applicant:

1. Has the legal authority to apply for Federal assistance, and the institutional, managerial and financial capability (including funds sufficient to pay the non-Federal share of project costs) to ensure proper planning, management and completion of the project described in this application.

2. Will give the awarding agency, the Comptroller General of the United States and, if appropriate, the State, through any authorized representative, access to and the right to examine all records, books, papers, or documents related to the assistance; and will establish a proper accounting system in accordance with generally accepted accounting standards or agency directives.

3. Will not dispose of, modify the use of, or change the terms of the real property title, or other interest in the site and facilities without permission and instructions from the awarding agency. Will record the Federal interest in the title of real property in accordance with awarding agency directives and will include a covenant in the title of real property aquired in whole or in part with Federal assistance funds to assure non-discrimination during the useful life of the project.

4. Will comply with the requirements of the assistance awarding agency with regard to the drafting, review and approval of construction plans and specifications.

5. Will provide and maintain competent and adequate engineering supervision at the construction site to ensure that the complete work conforms with the approved plans and specifications and will furnish progress reports and such other information as may be required by the assistance awarding agency or State.

6. Will initiate and complete the work within the applicable time frame after receipt of approval of the awarding agency.

7. Will establish safeguards to prohibit employees from using their positions for a purpose that constitutes or presents the appearance of personal or organizational conflict of interest, or personal gain.

8. Will comply with the Intergovernmental Personnel Act of 1970 (42 U.S.C. §§4728-4763) relating to prescribed standards for merit systems for programs funded under one of the 19 statutes or regulations specified in Appendix A of OPM's Standards for a Merit System of Personnel Administration (5 C.F.R. 900, Subpart F).

9. Will comply with the Lead-Based Paint Poisoning Prevention Act (42 U.S.C. §§4801 et seq.) which prohibits the use of lead-based paint in construction or rehabilitation of residence structures.

10. Will comply with all Federal statutes relating to non-discrimination. These include but are not limited to: (a) Title VI of the Civil Rights Act of 1964 (P.L. 88-352) which prohibits discrimination on the basis of race, color or national origin; (b) Title IX of the Education Amendments of 1972, as amended (20 U.S.C. §§1681 1683, and 1685-1686), which prohibits discrimination on the basis of sex; (c) Section 504 of the Rehabilitation Act of 1973, as amended (29 U.S.C. §794), which prohibits discrimination on the basis of handicaps; (d) the Age Discrimination Act of 1975, as amended (42 U.S.C. §§6101-6107), which prohibits discrimination on the basis of age; (e) the Drug Abuse Office and Treatment Act of 1972 (P.L. 92-255), as amended, relating to nondiscrimination on the basis of drug abuse; (f) the Comprehensive Alcohol Abuse and Alcoholism Prevention, Treatment and Rehabilitation Act of 1970 (P.L. 91-616), as amended, relating to nondiscrimination on the basis of alcohol abuse or alcoholism; (g) §§523 and 527 of the Public Health Service Act of 1912 (42 U.S.C. §§290 dd-3 and 290 ee 3), as amended, relating to confidentiality of alcohol and drug abuse patient records; (h) Title VIII of the Civil Rights Act of 1968 (42 U.S.C. §§3601 et seq.), as amended, relating to nondiscrimination in the sale, rental or financing of housing; (i) any other nondiscrimination provisions in the specific statute(s) under which application for Federal assistance is being made; and, (j) the requirements of any other nondiscrimination statute(s) which may apply to the application.

Standard Form 424D (Rev. 7-97)

Previous Edition Usable   Authorized for Local Reproduction   Prescribed by OMB Circular A-102

11. Will comply, or has already complied, with the requirements of Titles II and III of the Uniform Relocation Assistance and Real Property Acquisition Policies Act of 1970 (P.L. 91-646) which provide for fair and equitable treatment of persons displaced or whose property is acquired as a result of Federal and federally-assisted programs. These requirements apply to all interests in real property acquired for project purposes regardless of Federal participation in purchases.

12. Will comply with the provisions of the Hatch Act (5 U.S.C. §§1501-1508 and 7324-7328) which limit the political activities of employees whose principal employment activities are funded in whole or in part with Federal funds.

13. Will comply, as applicable, with the provisions of the Davis-Bacon Act (40 U.S.C. §§276a to 276a-7), the Copeland Act (40 U.S.C. §276c and 18 U.S.C. §874), and the Contract Work Hours and Safety Standards Act (40 U.S.C. §§327-333) regarding labor standards for federally-assisted construction subagreements.

14. Will comply with flood insurance purchase requirements of Section 102(a) of the Flood Disaster Protection Act of 1973 (P.L. 93-234) which requires recipients in a special flood hazard area to participate in the program and to purchase flood insurance if the total cost of insurable construction and acquisition is $10,000 or more.

15. Will comply with environmental standards which may be prescribed pursuant to the following: (a) institution of environmental quality control measures under the

National Environmental Policy Act of 1969 (P.L. 91-190) and Executive Order (EO) 11514; (b) notification of violating facilities pursuant to EO 11738; (c) protection of wetlands pursuant to EO 11990; (d) evaluation of flood hazards in floodplains in accordance with EO 11988; (e) assurance of project consistency with the approved State management program developed under the Coastal Zone Management Act of 1972 (16 U.S.C. §§1451 et seq.); (f) conformity of Federal actions to State (Clean Air) Implementation Plans under Section 176(c) of the Clean Air Act of 1955, as amended (42 U.S.C. §§7401 et seq.); (g) protection of underground sources of drinking water under the Safe Drinking Water Act of 1974, as amended (P.L. 93-523); and, (h) protection of endangered species under the Endangered Species Act of 1973, as amended (P.L. 93-205).

16. Will comply with the Wild and Scenic Rivers Act of 1968 (16 U.S.C. §§1271 et seq.) related to protecting components or potential components of the national wild and scenic rivers system.

17. Will assist the awarding agency in assuring compliance with Section 106 of the National Historic Preservation Act of 1966, as amended (16 U.S.C. §470), EO 11593 (identification and protection of historic properties), and the Archaeological and Historic Preservation Act of 1974 (16 U.S.C. §§469a-1 et seq.).

18. Will cause to be performed the required financial and compliance audits in accordance with the Single Audit Act Amendments of 1996 and OMB Circular No. A-133, "Audits of States, Local Governments, and Non-Profit Organizations."

19. Will comply with all applicable requirements of all other Federal laws, executive orders, regulations, and policies governing this program.

SIGNATURE OF AUTHORIZED CERTIFYING OFFICIAL	TITLE
APPLICANT ORGANIZATION	DATE SUBMITTED

SF-424D (Rev. 7-97) Back

Standard Form LLL

DISCLOSURE OF LOBBYING ACTIVITIES

Complete this form to disclose lobbying activities pursuant to 31 U.S.C. 1352
(See reverse for public burden disclosure.)

1. Type of Federal Action:
    a. contract
    b. grant
    c. cooperative agreement
    d. loan
    e. loan guarantee
    f. loan insurance

2. Status of Federal Action:
    a. bid/offer/application
    b. initial award
    c. post-award

3. Report Type:
    a. initial/filing
    b. material change

For Material Change Only:

    year _____ quarter _____
    date of last report _____

4. Name and Address of Reporting Entity:

    ☐ Prime   ☐ Subawardee
                         Tier _____, *if known:*

Congressional District, *if known:*

5. If Reporting Entity in No. 4 is Subawardee, Enter Name and Address of Prime:

Congressional District, *if known:*

6. Federal Department/Agency:

7. Federal Program Name/Description:

CFDA Number, *if applicable:* _____

8. Federal Action Number, if known:

9. Award Amount, if known:
$

10. a. Name and Address of Lobbying Registrant
(if individual, last name, first name, MI):

b. Individuals Performing Services *(including address if different from No. 10a)*
(last name, first name, MI):

[ITEMS 11-15 REMOVED]

16. Information requested through this form is authorized by title 31 U.S.C. section 1352. This disclosure of lobbying activities is a material representation of fact upon which reliance was placed by the tier above when this transaction was made or entered into. This disclosure is required pursuant to 31 U.S.C. 1352. This information will be reported to the Congress semi-annually and will be available for public inspection. Any person who fails to file the required disclosure shall be subject to a civil penalty of not less than $10,000 and not more than $100,000 for each such failure.

Signature: _____

Print Name: _____

Title: _____

Telephone No.: _____ Date: _____

Federal Use Only:

Authorized for Local Reproduction
Standard Form-LLL

INSTRUCTIONS FOR COMPLETION OF SF-LLL, DISCLOSURE OF LOBBYING ACTIVITIES

This disclosure form shall be completed by the reporting entity, whether subawardee or prime federal recipient, at the initiation or receipt of a covered federal action, or a material change to a previous filing, pursuant to title 31 U.S.C. section 1352. The filing of a form is required for each payment or agreement to make payment to any lobbying entity for influencing or attempting to influence an officer or employee of any agency, a member of Congress, an officer or employee of Congress, or an employee of a member of Congress in connection with a covered federal action. Complete all items that apply for both the initial filing and material change report. Refer to the implementing guidance published by the Office of Management and Budget for additional information.

1. Identify the type of covered federal action for which lobbying activity is and/or has been secured to influence the outcome of a covered federal action.

2. Identify the status of the covered federal action.

3. Identify the appropriate classification of this report. If this is a followup report caused by a material change to the information previously reported, enter the year and quarter in which the change occurred. Enter the date of the last previously submitted report by this reporting entity for this covered federal action.

4. Enter the full name, address, city, state and zip code of the reporting entity. Include congressional district, if known. Check the appropriate classification of the reporting entity that designates if it is, or expects to be, a prime or subaward recipient. Identify the tier of the subawardee, e.g., the first subawardee of the prime is the 1st tier. Subawards include but are not limited to subcontracts, subgrants and contract awards under grants.

5. If the organization filing the report in item 4 checks "Subawardee," then enter the full name, address, city, state and zip code of the prime federal recipient. Include congressional district, if known.

6. Enter the name of the federal agency making the award or loan commitment. Include at least one organizational level below agency name, if known. For example, Department of Transportation, United States Coast Guard.

7. Enter the federal program name or description for the covered federal action (item 1). If known, enter the full Catalog of Federal Domestic Assistance (CFDA) number for grants, cooperative agreements, loans, and loan commitments.

8. Enter the most appropriate federal identifying number available for the federal action identified in item 1 (e.g., Request for Proposal (RFP) number; Invitation for Bid (IFB) number; grant announcement number; the contract, grant, or loan award number; the application/ proposal control number assigned by the federal agency). Include prefixes, e.g., "RFP-DE-90-001."

9. For a covered federal action where there has been an award or loan commitment by the federal agency, enter the federal amount of the award/loan commitment for the prime entity identified in item 4 or 5.

10. (a) Enter the full name, address, city, state and zip code of the registrant under the Lobbying Disclosure Act of 1995 engaged by the reporting entity identified in item 1 to influence the covered federal action.

   (b) Enter the full names of the individual(s) performing services, and include full address if different from 10(a). Enter Last Name, First Name, and   Middle Initial (MI).

[ITEMS 11-15 REMOVED]

16. The certifying official shall sign and date the form, print his/her name, title, and telephone number.

Public reporting burden for this collection of information is estimated to average 30 minutes per response, including time for reviewing instructions, searching existing data sources, gathering and maintaining the data needed, and completing and reviewing the collection of information. Send comments regarding the burden estimate or any other aspect of this collection of information, including suggestions for reducing this burden, to the Office of Management and Budget, Paperwork Reduction Project (0348-0046), Washington, D.C. 20503.

Certification Regarding Debarment, Suspension, Ineligibility and Voluntary Exclusion — Lower Tier Covered Transactions

Instructions for Certification

1. By signing and submitting this proposal, the prospective lower tier participant is providing the certification set out below.

2. The certification in this clause is a material representation of fact upon which reliance was placed when this transaction was entered into. If it is later determined that the prospective lower tier participant knowingly rendered an erroneous certification, in addition to other remedies available to the Federal Government, the department or agency with which this transaction originated may pursue available remedies, including suspension and/or debarment.

3. The prospective lower tier participant shall provide immediate written notice to the person to which this proposal is submitted if at any time the prospective lower tier participant learns that its certification was erroneous when submitted or has become erroneous by reason of changed circumstances.

4. The terms "covered transaction," "debarred," "suspended," "ineligible," "lower tier covered transaction," "participant," " person," "primary covered transaction," "principal," "proposal," and "voluntarily excluded," as used in this clause, have the meanings set out in the Definitions and Coverage sections of rules implementing Executive Order 12549. You may contact the person to which this proposal is submitted for assistance in obtaining a copy of those regulations.

5. The prospective lower tier participant agrees by submitting this proposal that, should the proposed covered transaction be entered into, it shall not knowingly enter into any lower tier covered transaction with a person who is debarred, suspended, declared ineligible, or voluntarily excluded from participation in this covered transaction, unless authorized by the department or agency with which this transaction originated.

6. The prospective lower tier participant further agrees by submitting this proposal that it will include the clause titled A Certification Regarding Debarment, Suspension, Ineligibility, and Voluntary Exclusion-Lower Tier Covered Transactions, without modification, in all lower tier covered transactions and in all solicitations for lower tier covered transactions.

7. A participant in a covered transaction may rely upon a certification of a prospective participant in a lower tier covered transaction that it is not debarred, suspended, ineligible, or voluntarily excluded from the covered transaction, unless it knows that the certification is erroneous. A participant may decide the method and frequency by which it determines the eligibility of its principals. Each participant may but is not required to, check the Nonprocurement List.

8. Nothing contained in the foregoing shall be construed to require establishment of a system of records in order to render in good faith the certification required by this clause. The knowledge and information of a participant is not required to exceed that which is normally possessed by a prudent person in the ordinary course of business dealings.

9. Except for transactions authorized under paragraph 5 of these instructions, if a participant in a covered transaction knowingly enters into a lower tier covered transaction with a person who is suspended, debarred, ineligible, or voluntarily excluded from participation in this transaction, in addition to other remedies available to the Federal Government, the department or agency with which this transaction originated may pursue available remedies, including suspension and/or debarment.

Certification

(1) The prospective lower tier participant certifies, by submission of this proposal, that neither it nor its principals are presently debarred, suspended, proposed for debarment, declared ineligible, or voluntarily excluded from participation in this transaction by any Federal department or agency.

(2) Where the prospective lower tier participant is unable to certify to any of the statements in this certification, such prospective participant shall attach an explanation to this proposal.

NAME OF APPLICANT	PR/AWARD NUMBER AND/OR PROJECT NAME
PRINTED NAME AND TITLE OF AUTHORIZED REPRESENTATIVE	
SIGNATURE	DATE

CERTIFICATION REGARDING DRUG-FREE WORKPLACE REQUIREMENTS

DRUG-FREE WORKPLACE (GRANTEES OTHER THAN INDIVIDUALS)

As required by the Drug-Free Workplace Act of 1988—

A. The applicant certifies that it will or will continue to provide a drug-free workplace by:

(a) Publishing a statement notifying employees that the unlawful manufacture, distribution, dispensing, possession, or use of a controlled substance is prohibited in the grantee's workplace and specifying the actions that will be taken against employees for violation of such prohibition;

(b) Establishing an on-going drug-free awareness program to inform employees about:

(1) The dangers of drug abuse in the workplace;

(2) The grantee's policy of maintaining a drug-free workplace;

(3) Any available drug counseling, rehabilitation, and employee assistance programs; and

(4) The penalties that may be imposed upon employees for drug abuse violations occurring in the workplace;

(c) Making it a requirement that each employee to be engaged in the performance of the grant be given a copy of the statement required by paragraph (a);

(d) Notifying the employee in the statement required by paragraph (a) that, as a condition of employment under the grant, the employee will:

(1) Abide by the terms of the statement; and

(2) Notify the employer in writing of his or her conviction for a violation of a criminal drug statute occurring in the workplace no later than five calendar days after such conviction;

(e) Notifying the agency, in writing, within 10 calendar days after receiving notice under subparagraph (d)(2) from an employee or otherwise receiving actual notice of such conviction. Employers of convicted employees must provide notice, including position title, to: Director, Grants Policy and Oversight Staff, U.S. Department of Education, 400 Maryland Avenue, S.W. (Room 3652, GSA Regional Office Building No. 3), Washington, DC 20202-4248. Notice shall include the identification number(s) of each affected grant;

(f) Taking one of the following actions, within 30 calendar days of receiving notice under subparagraph (d)(2), with respect to any employee who is so convicted:

(1) Taking appropriate personnel action against such an employee, up to and including termination, consistent with the requirements of the Rehabilitation Act of 1973, as amended; or

(2) Requiring such employee to participate satisfactorily in a drug abuse assistance or rehabilitation program approved for such purposes by a Federal, State, or local health, law enforcement, or other appropriate agency;

(g) Making a good faith effort to continue to maintain a drug-free workplace through implementation of paragraphs (a), (b), (c), (d), (e), and (f).

B. The grantee may insert in the space provided below the site(s) for the performance of work done in connection with the specific grant:

Place of Performance (Street address. city, county, state, zip code)

Check [ ] if there are workplaces on file that are not identified here.

Certification

As the duly authorized representative of the applicant, I hereby certify that the applicant will comply with the above certifications.

NAME OF APPLICANT	PR/AWARD NUMBER AND/OR PROJECT NAME
PRINTED NAME AND TITLE OF AUTHORIZED REPRESENTATIVE	
SIGNATURE	DATE

8 | Resources for Grantseekers

Sources of Information on Private Sector Grants

Discovering which private foundations and corporate givers are currently inviting applications, which grantmakers fit your organization's funding needs and what application procedures and guidelines exist can be a challenging task. But there are numerous resources that can help you keep track of what is going on in the world of private sector grants.

➢ **The Foundation Center.** This nonprofit organization is an independent, national service entity created by foundations. It offers a wide array of resources and services that may be useful to grantseekers searching for information on private giving. Several of The Foundation Center's publications and online resources may be useful in researching private givers, their priorities and grantmaking guidelines. Following are two examples of the organization's publications.

The *Foundation Directory* is one of the most comprehensive sources of general information on the largest foundations. It includes facts and figures on nearly 8,000 foundations worldwide. Each listing includes information such as foundation purpose and activities, financial data, names of officers and trustees, and contact information.

The *Foundation Grants Index* lists recently awarded grants of more than $10,000. The *Index* lists grants by state and by foundation and also indexes them by type of recipient, key words, location, type of support and subject.

The Foundation Center disseminates information through a national network of "Cooperating Collections." Participants in the Foundation Center's Cooperating Collections network are libraries or nonprofit information centers that provide fundraising information and other funding-related technical assistance in their communities. Cooperating Collections agree to provide free public access to a basic collection of Foundation Center publications during a regular schedule of hours, offering free funding research guidance to all visitors. Many also provide a variety of services for local nonprofit organizations, using staff or volunteers to prepare special materials, organize workshops, or conduct orientations.

The Cooperating Collections, located throughout the country, maintain a core collection of Foundation Center publications and a variety of supplementary materials and services in areas useful to grantseekers. The core collection consists of:

> *The Foundation Directory*
>
> *The Foundation Directory Part 2*
>
> *The Foundation Directory Supplement*
>
> *The Foundation 1000*
>
> *Foundation Fundamentals*
>
> *Foundation Giving*
>
> *The Foundation Grants Index*
>
> *The Foundation Grants Index Quarterly*
>
> *Foundation Grants to Individuals*

Guide to U.S. Foundations, Their Trustees, Officers, and Donors
The Foundation Center's Guide to Proposal Writing
National Directory of Corporate Giving
National Directory of Grantmaking Public Charities
National Guide to Funding... (series)
The Foundation Center's User-Friendly Guide

Many Cooperating Collections make available for public use sets of private foundation information returns (IRS Form 990–PF). Collections marked with an asterisk (*) have available those information returns for their state and/or neighboring states. A complete set of U.S. foundation returns can be found at the New York and Washington, D.C., offices of the Foundation Center. The Atlanta, Cleveland, and San Francisco offices have IRS Form 990–PF returns for the Southeastern, Midwestern, and Western states, respectively.

The Cooperating Collections, listed below, are arranged alphabetically by the city or community in which they are located. Many of the Cooperating Collections also have available the Foundation Center's Database on CD–ROM. It is recommended that you call the collection in advance of a visit to determine hours and availability of the Foundation Center's Database on CD–ROM.

Additional information about the Foundation Center, its publications or services is available from The Foundation Center, 79 Fifth Ave., 8th Floor, New York, NY 10003; (212) 620–4230. Visit the center online at **http://www.foundationcenter.org**.

Foundation Center Cooperating Collection Centers

ALABAMA

*BIRMINGHAM PUBLIC LIBRARY
Government Documents
2100 Park Place
Birmingham 35203
(205) 226–3620

HUNTSVILLE PUBLIC LIBRARY
915 Monroe St.
Huntsville 35801
(256) 532–5940

*UNIVERSITY OF SOUTH ALABAMA
Library Building
Mobile 36688
(334) 460–7025

AUBURN UNIVERSITY AT MONTGOMERY
LIBRARY
7300 University Drive
Montgomery 36124–4023
(334) 244–3200

ALASKA

*UNIVERSITY OF ALASKA AT ANCHORAGE
LIBRARY
3211 Providence Drive
Anchorage 99508
(907) 786–1847

JUNEAU PUBLIC LIBRARY
Reference
292 Marine Way
Juneau 99801
(907) 586–5267

ARIZONA

*PHOENIX PUBLIC LIBRARY
Information Services Department
1221 N. Central
Phoenix 85004
(602) 262–4636

*TUCSON-PIMA LIBRARY
101 N. Stone Ave.
Tucson 87501
(520) 791–4010

ARKANSAS

WESTARK COMMUNITY COLLEGE-BORHAM
   LIBRARY
5210 Grand Ave.
Fort Smith 72913
(501) 788-7200

*CENTRAL ARKANSAS LIBRARY SYSTEM
100 Rock St.
Little Rock 72201
(501) 918-3000

PINE BLUFF-JEFFERSON COUNTY LIBRARY
   SYSTEM
200 E. Eighth
Pine Bluff 71601
(870) 534-2159

CALIFORNIA

HUMBOLDT AREA FOUNDATION
P.O. Box 99
Bayside 95524
(707) 442-2993

*VENTURA COUNTY COMMUNITY
   FOUNDATION
Resource Center for Nonprofit Organizations
1317 Del Norte Road, Suite 150
Camarillo 93010-8504
(805) 988-0196

FRESNO REGIONAL FOUNDATION
Nonprofit Advancement Center
1999 Tuolumne St., Suite 650
Fresno 93720
(559) 498-3929

CENTER FOR NONPROFIT MANAGEMENT
   IN SOUTHERN CALIFORNIA
Nonprofit Resource Library
315 W. Ninth St., Suite 1100
Los Angeles 90015
(213) 623-7080

FLINTRIDGE FOUNDATION
Philanthropy Resource Library
1040 Lincoln Ave., Suite 100
Pasadena 91103
(626) 449-0839

*GRANT & RESOURCE CENTER OF
   NORTHERN CALIFORNIA
Building C, Suite A
2280 Benton Dr.
Redding 96003
(530) 244-1219

LOS ANGELES PUBLIC LIBRARY
West Valley Regional Branch Library
19036 Van Owen St.
Reseda 91335
(818) 345-4393

RIVERSIDE PUBLIC LIBRARY
3581 Mission Inn Ave.
Riverside 92501
(909) 782-5202

*NONPROFIT RESOURCE CENTER
Sacramento Public Library
828 I St., 2nd Floor
Sacramento 95814
(916) 264-2772

SAN DIEGO FOUNDATION
Funding Information Center
1420 Kettner Blvd., Suite 500
San Diego 92101
(619) 239-8815

*SAN FRANCISCO FIELD OFFICE AND LIBRARY
312 Sutter St., Room 312
San Francisco 94108
(415) 397-0902

*NONPROFIT DEVELOPMENT CENTER
Library
1922 The Alameda, Suite 212
San Jose 95126
(408) 248-9505

*PENINSULA COMMUNITY FOUNDATION
Peninsula Nonprofit Center
1700 S. El Camino Real, Room 201
San Mateo 94402-3049
(650) 358-9392

LOS ANGELES PUBLIC LIBRARY
San Pedro Regional Branch
9131 S. Gaffey St.
San Pedro 90731
(310) 548-7779

*VOLUNTEER CENTER OF ORANGE COUNTY
Nonprofit Management Assistance Center
1901 E. Fourth St., Suite 100
Santa Ana 92705
(714) 953-5757

*SANTA BARBARA PUBLIC LIBRARY
40 E. Anapamu St.
Santa Barbara 93101-1019
(805) 564-5633

SANTA MONICA PUBLIC LIBRARY
1343 Sixth St.
Santa Monica 90401-1603
(310) 458-8600

SONOMA COUNTY LIBRARY
Third & E streets
Santa Rosa 95404
(707) 545-0831

SEASIDE BRANCH LIBRARY
550 Harcourt St.
Seaside 93955
(408) 899-8131

SONORA AREA FOUNDATION
20100 Cedar Road N.
Sonora 95370
(209) 533-2596

COLORADO

EL POMAR NONPROFIT RESOURCE LIBRARY
1661 Mesa Ave.
Colorado Springs 80906
(719) 577-7000

*DENVER PUBLIC LIBRARY
General Reference
10 W. 14th Ave. Parkway
Denver 80204
(303) 640-6200

CONNECTICUT

DANBURY PUBLIC LIBRARY
170 Main St.
Danbury 06810
(203) 797-4527

*GREENWICH PUBLIC LIBRARY
101 W. Putnam Ave.
Greenwich 06830
(203) 622-7900

*HARTFORD PUBLIC LIBRARY
500 Main St.
Hartford 06103
(860) 543-8656

*NEW HAVEN FREE PUBLIC LIBRARY
Reference Department
133 Elm St.
New Haven 06510-2057
(203) 946-8130

DELAWARE

*UNIVERSITY OF DELAWARE
Hugh Morris Library
Newark 19717-5267
(302) 831-2432

DISTRICT OF COLUMBIA

*FOUNDATION CENTER OFFICE AND LIBRARY
1001 Connecticut Ave. N.W.
Suite 938
Washington 20036
(202) 331-1400

FLORIDA

VOLUSIA COUNTY LIBRARY CENTER
City Island
105 E. Magnolia Ave.
Daytona Beach 32114-4484
(904) 257-6036

*NOVA SOUTHEASTERN UNIVERSITY
Einstein Library
3301 College Ave.
Fort Lauderdale 33314
(954) 262-4601

INDIAN RIVER COMMUNITY COLLEGE
Learning Resources Center
3209 Virginia Ave.
Fort Pierce 34981-5596
(561) 462-4757

*JACKSONVILLE PUBLIC LIBRARIES
Grants Resource Center
122 N. Ocean St.
Jacksonville 32202
(904) 630-2665

*MIAMI-DADE PUBLIC LIBRARY
Humanities/Social Science
101 W. Flagler St.
Miami 33130
(305) 375-5575

ORANGE COUNTY LIBRARY SYSTEM
Social Sciences Department
101 E. Central Blvd.
Orlando 32801
(407) 425-4694

SELBY PUBLIC LIBRARY
Reference
1331 First St.
Sarasota 34236
(941) 316-1183

*TAMPA-HILLSBOROUGH COUNTY PUBLIC
  LIBRARY
900 N. Ashley Drive
Tampa 33602
(813) 273-3652

*COMMUNITY FOUNDATION OF PALM BEACH
& MARTIN COUNTIES
324 Datura St., Suite 340
West Palm Beach 33401
(561) 659-6800

GEORGIA

*ATLANTA FIELD OFFICE AND LIBRARY
Suite 150, Grand Lobby
Hurt Building, 50 Hurt Plaza
Atlanta 30303-2914
(404) 880-0094

ATLANTA-FULTON PUBLIC LIBRARY
Foundation Collection–Ivan Allen Department
1 Margaret Mitchell Square
Atlanta 30303-1089
(404) 730-1900

UNITED WAY OF CENTRAL GEORGIA
Community Resource Center
277 Martin Luther King Jr. Blvd., Suite 301
Macon 31201
(912) 745-4732

SAVANNAH STATE UNIVERSITY
Asa Gordon Library
P.O. Box 20394
Savannah 31404
(912) 356-2185

THOMAS COUNTY PUBLIC LIBRARY
201 N. Madison St.
Thomasville 31792
(912) 225-5252

HAWAII

*UNIVERSITY OF HAWAII
Hamilton Library
2550 The Mall
Honolulu 96822
(808) 956-7214

HAWAII COMMUNITY FOUNDATION
  FUNDING RESOURCE LIBRARY
900 Fort St., Suite 1300
Honolulu 96813
(808) 537-6333

IDAHO

BOISE PUBLIC LIBRARY
715 S. Capitol Blvd.
Boise 83702
(208) 384-4024

*CALDWELL PUBLIC LIBRARY
1010 Dearborn St.
Caldwell 83605
(208) 459-3242

ILLINOIS

*DONORS FORUM OF CHICAGO
208 S. LaSalle, Suite 735
Chicago 60604
(312) 578-0175

*EVANSTON PUBLIC LIBRARY
1703 Orrington Ave.
Evanston 60201
(847) 866-0305

ROCK ISLAND PUBLIC LIBRARY
401 19th St.
Rock Island 61201
(309) 788-7627

UNIVERSITY OF ILLINOIS AT SPRINGFIELD
Brookens Library
Shepherd Road
Springfield 62794-9243
(217) 206-6633

INDIANA

*EVANSVILLE-VANDERBURGH COUNTY
PUBLIC LIBRARY
22 S.E. Fifth St.
Evansville 47708
(812) 428-8200

*ALLEN COUNTY PUBLIC LIBRARY
900 Webster St.
Fort Wayne 46802
(219) 421–1200

*INDIANAPOLIS-MARION COUNTY PUBLIC
LIBRARY
Social Sciences
40 E. St. Clair
Indianapolis 46206
(317) 269–1733

*VIGO COUNTY PUBLIC LIBRARY
1 Library Square
Terre Haute 47807
(812) 232–1113

IOWA

CEDAR RAPIDS PUBLIC LIBRARY
Foundation Center Collection
500 First St. S.E.
Cedar Rapids 52401
(319) 398–5123

SOUTHWESTERN COMMUNITY COLLEGE
Learning Resource Center
1501 W. Townline Road
Creston 50801
(515) 782–7081

PUBLIC LIBRARY OF DES MOINES
100 Locust
Des Moines 50309–1791
(515) 283–4152

SIOUX CITY PUBLIC LIBRARY
529 Pierce St.
Sioux City 51101–1202
(712) 252–5669

KANSAS

*DODGE CITY PUBLIC LIBRARY
1001 Second Ave.
Dodge City 67801
(316) 225–0248

*TOPEKA AND SHAWNEE COUNTY PUBLIC
LIBRARY
1515 S.W. 10th Ave.
Topeka 66604–1374
(785) 233–2040

*WICHITA PUBLIC LIBRARY
223 S. Main St.
Wichita 67202
(316) 261–8500

KENTUCKY

WESTERN KENTUCKY UNIVERSITY
Helm-Cravens Library
Bowling Green 42101–3576
(502) 745–6125

*LEXINGTON PUBLIC LIBRARY
140 E. Main St.
Lexington 40507–1376
(606) 231–5520

*LOUISVILLE FREE PUBLIC LIBRARY
301 York St.
Louisville 40203
(502) 574–1611

LOUISIANA

*EAST BATON ROUGE PARISH LIBRARY
Centroplex Branch Grants Collection
120 St. Louis
Baton Rouge 70802
(504) 389–4960

BEAUREGARD PARISH LIBRARY
205 S. Washington Ave.
De Ridder 70634
(318) 463–6217

OUACHITA PARISH PUBLIC LIBRARY
1800 Stubbs Ave.
Monroe 71201
(318) 327–1490

*NEW ORLEANS PUBLIC LIBRARY
Business & Science Division
219 Loyola Ave.
New Orleans 70140
(504) 596–2580

*SHREVE MEMORIAL LIBRARY
424 Texas St.
Shreveport 71120–1523
(318) 226–5894

MAINE

MAINE GRANTS INFORMATION CENTER
University of Southern Maine Library
314 Forrest Ave.
Portland 04104–9301
(207) 780–5039

MARYLAND

*ENOCH PRATT FREE LIBRARY
Social Science & History
400 Cathedral St.
Baltimore 21201
(410) 396–5430

MASSACHUSETTS

*ASSOCIATED GRANTMAKERS OF
    MASSACHUSETTS
294 Washington St., Suite 840
Boston 02108
(617) 426–2606

*BOSTON PUBLIC LIBRARY
Social Science Reference
700 Boylston St.
Boston 02117
(617) 536–5400

WESTERN MASSACHUSETTS FUNDING
    RESOURCE CENTER
65 Elliot St.
Springfield 01101–1730
(413) 732–3175

*WORCESTER PUBLIC LIBRARY
Grants Resource Center
Salem Square
Worcester 01608
(508) 799–1655

MICHIGAN

ALPENA COUNTY LIBRARY
211 N. First St.
Alpena 49707
(517) 356–6188

*UNIVERSITY OF MICHIGAN–ANN ARBOR
Graduate Library
Reference & Research Services Department
Ann Arbor 48109–1205
(313) 764–9373

WILLARD PUBLIC LIBRARY
Nonprofit and Funding Resource Collections
7 W. Van Buren St.
Battle Creek 49017
(616) 968–8166

*HENRY FORD CENTENNIAL LIBRARY
Adult Services
16301 Michigan Ave.
Dearborn 48124
(313) 943–2330

*WAYNE STATE UNIVERSITY
Purdy/Kresge Library
5265 Cass Ave.
Detroit 48202
(313) 577–6424

*MICHIGAN STATE UNIVERSITY LIBRARIES
Social Sciences/Humanities
Main Library
East Lansing 48824–1048
(517) 353–8818

*FARMINGTON COMMUNITY LIBRARY
32737 W. 12 Mile Road
Farmington Hills 48334
(248) 553–0300

*UNIVERSITY OF MICHIGAN–FLINT
Library
Flint 48502–2186
(810) 762–3408

*GRAND RAPIDS PUBLIC LIBRARY
Business Department, 3rd Floor
60 Library Plaza N.E.
Grand Rapids 49503–3093
(616) 456–3600

MICHIGAN TECHNOLOGICAL UNIVERSITY
Van Pelt Library
1400 Townsend Dr.
Houghton 49931
(906) 487–2507

MAUD PRESTON PALENSKE MEMORIAL
    LIBRARY
500 Market St.
St. Joseph 49085
(616) 983–7167

*NORTHWESTERN MICHIGAN COLLEGE
Mark & Helen Osterin Library
1701 E. Front St.
Traverse City 49684
(616) 922-1060

MINNESOTA

*DULUTH PUBLIC LIBRARY
520 W. Superior St.
Duluth 55802
(218) 723-3802

SOUTHWEST STATE UNIVERSITY
University Library
North Highway 23
Marshall 56253
(507) 537-6176

*MINNEAPOLIS PUBLIC LIBRARY
Sociology Department
300 Nicollet Mall
Minneapolis 55401
(612) 630-6300

ROCHESTER PUBLIC LIBRARY
101 Second St. S.E.
Rochester 55904-3777
(507) 285-8002

ST. PAUL PUBLIC LIBRARY
90 W. Fourth St.
St. Paul 55102
(651) 266-7000

MISSISSIPPI

*JACKSON/HINDS LIBRARY SYSTEM
300 N. State St.
Jackson 39201
(601) 968-5803

MISSOURI

*CLEARINGHOUSE FOR MIDCONTINENT
FOUNDATIONS
University of Missouri
5110 Cherry, Suite 310
Kansas City 64110
(816) 235-1176

*KANSAS CITY PUBLIC LIBRARY
311 E. 12th St.
Kansas City 64106
(816) 701-3541

*METROPOLITAN ASSOCIATION FOR
PHILANTHROPY INC.
1 Metropolitan Square
211 N. Broadway, Suite 1200
St. Louis 63102
(314) 621-6220

*SPRINGFIELD-GREENE COUNTY LIBRARY
397 E. Central
Springfield 65802
(417) 837-5000

MONTANA

*MONTANA STATE UNIVERSITY - BILLINGS
Library - Special Collections
1500 N. 30th St.
Billings 59101-0298
(406) 657-2046

*BOZEMAN PUBLIC LIBRARY
220 E. Lamme
Bozeman 59715
(406) 582-2402

*MONTANA STATE LIBRARY
Library Services
1515 E. Sixth Ave.
Helena 59620
(406) 444-3004

*UNIVERSITY OF MONTANA
Maureen & Mike Mansfield Library
Missoula 59812-1195
(406) 243-6800

NEBRASKA

UNIVERSITY OF NEBRASKA-LINCOLN
Love Library
14th & R streets
Lincoln 68588-0410
(402) 472-2848

*W. DALE CLARK LIBRARY
Social Sciences Department
215 S. 15th St.
Omaha 68102
(402) 444-4826

NEVADA

CLARK COUNTY LIBRARY
1401 E. Flamingo
Las Vegas 89119
(702) 733-3642

*WASHOE COUNTY LIBRARY
301 S. Center St.
Reno 89501
(702) 785–4010

NEW HAMPSHIRE

*CONCORD PUBLIC LIBRARY
45 Green St.
Concord 03301
(603) 225–8670

*PLYMOUTH STATE COLLEGE
Herbert H. Lamson Library
Plymouth 03264
(603) 535–2258

NEW JERSEY

CUMBERLAND COUNTY LIBRARY
800 E. Commerce St.
Bridgeton 08302
(609) 453–2210

FREE PUBLIC LIBRARY OF ELIZABETH
11 S. Broad St.
Elizabeth 07202
(908) 354–6060

*COUNTY COLLEGE OF MORRIS
Learning Resource Center
214 Center Grove Road
Randolph 07869
(973) 328–5296

*NEW JERSEY STATE LIBRARY
Governmental Reference Services
185 W. State St.
Trenton 08625–0520
(609) 292–6220

NEW MEXICO

ALBUQUERQUE COMMUNITY FOUNDATION
3301 Menaul N.E., Suite 30
Albuquerque 87176–6960
(505) 883–6240

*NEW MEXICO STATE LIBRARY
Information Services
1209 Camino Carlos Rey
Santa Fe 87505–9860
(505) 476–9714

NEW YORK

NEW YORK STATE LIBRARY
Humanities Reference
Cultural Education Center, 6th floor
Empire State Plaza
Albany 12230
(518) 474–5355

SUFFOLK COOPERATIVE LIBRARY SYSTEM
627 N. Sunrise Service Road
Bellport 11713
(516) 286–1600

NEW YORK PUBLIC LIBRARY
Bronx Reference Center
2556 Bainbridge Ave.
Bronx 10458–4698
(718) 579–4257

THE NONPROFIT CONNECTION INC.
1 Hanson Place, Room 2504
Brooklyn 11243
(718) 230–3200

BROOKLYN PUBLIC LIBRARY
Social Sciences/Philosophy Division
Grand Army Plaza
Brooklyn 11238
(718) 230–2122

*BUFFALO & ERIE COUNTY PUBLIC LIBRARY
Business, Science and Technology Dept.
1 Lafayette Square
Buffalo 14203
(716) 858–7097

HUNTINGTON PUBLIC LIBRARY
338 Main St.
Huntington 11743
(516) 427–5165

QUEENS BOROUGH PUBLIC LIBRARY
Social Sciences Division
89-11 Merrick Blvd.
Jamaica 11432
(718) 990–0700

*LEVITTOWN PUBLIC LIBRARY
1 Bluegrass Lane
Levittown 11756
(516) 731–5728

*FOUNDATION CENTER OFFICE AND LIBRARY
79 Fifth Ave.
2nd Floor
New York 10003-3076
(212) 620-4230

NEW YORK PUBLIC LIBRARY
Countee Cullen Branch Library
104 W. 136th St.
New York 10030
(212) 491-2070

ADRIANCE MEMORIAL LIBRARY
Special Services Department
93 Market St.
Poughkeepsie 12601
(914) 485-3445

ROCHESTER PUBLIC LIBRARY
Social Sciences
115 South Ave.
Rochester 14604
(716) 428-8128

ONONDAGA COUNTY PUBLIC LIBRARY
447 S. Salina St.
Syracuse 13202-2494
(315) 435-1900

UTICA PUBLIC LIBRARY
303 Genesee St.
Utica 13501
(315) 735-2279

*WHITE PLAINS PUBLIC LIBRARY
100 Martine Ave.
White Plains 10601
(914) 422-1480

NORTH CAROLINA

*COMMUNITY FOUNDATION OF WESTERN
  NORTH CAROLINA
Learning Resources Center
16 Biltmore Ave., Suite 201
P.O. Box 1888
Asheville 28802
(704) 254-4960

*THE DUKE ENDOWMENT
100 N. Tryon St., Suite 3500
Charlotte 28202
(704) 376-0291

DURHAM COUNTY PUBLIC LIBRARY
301 North Roxboro
Durham 27702
(919) 560-0110

*STATE LIBRARY OF NORTH CAROLINA
Government and Business Services
Archives Building
109 E. Jones St.
Raleigh 27601
(919) 733-3270

*FORSYTH COUNTY PUBLIC LIBRARY
660 W. Fifth St.
Winston-Salem 27101
(336) 727-2680

NORTH DAKOTA

BISMARCK PUBLIC LIBRARY
515 N. Fifth St.
Bismarck 58501
(701) 222-6410

*FARGO PUBLIC LIBRARY
102 N. Third St.
Fargo 58102
(701) 241-1491

OHIO

STARK COUNTY DISTRICT LIBRARY
Humanities
715 Market Ave. N.
Canton 44702
(330) 452-0665

*FOUNDATION CENTER OFFICE AND LIBRARY
Kent H. Smith Library
1422 Euclid Ave., Suite 1356
Cleveland 44115
(216) 861-1933

*PUBLIC LIBRARY OF CINCINNATI &
  HAMILTON COUNTY
Grants Resource Center
800 Vine St., Library Square
Cincinnati 45202-2071
(513) 369-6940

COLUMBUS METROPOLITAN LIBRARY
Business and Technology Dept.
96 S. Grant Ave.
Columbus 43215
(614) 645-2590

*DAYTON & MONTGOMERY COUNTY PUBLIC
   LIBRARY
Grants Resource Center
215 E. Third St.
Dayton 45402
(937) 227-9500 x211

MANSFIELD/RICHLAND COUNTY PUBLIC
   LIBRARY
42 W. Third St.
Mansfield 44902
(419) 521-3110

*TOLEDO-LUCAS COUNTY PUBLIC LIBRARY
Social Sciences Department
325 Michigan St.
Toledo 43624-1614
(419) 259-5245

*PUBLIC LIBRARY OF YOUNGSTOWN
   & MAHONING COUNTY LIBRARY
305 Wick Ave.
Youngstown 44503
(330) 744-8636

MUSKINGUM COUNTY LIBRARY
220 N. Fifth St.
Zanesville 43701
(614) 453-0391

OKLAHOMA

*OKLAHOMA CITY UNIVERSITY
Dulaney Browne Library
2501 N. Blackwelder
Oklahoma City 73106
(405) 521-5822

*TULSA CITY-COUNTY LIBRARY
400 Civic Center
Tulsa 74103
(918) 596-7940

OREGON

OREGON INSTITUTE OF TECHNOLOGY
Library
3201 Campus Dr.
Klamath Falls 97601-8801
(541) 885-1780

PACIFIC NONPROFIT NETWORK
Grantsmanship Resource Library
33 N. Central, Suite 211
Medford 97501
(503) 779-6044

*MULTNOMAH COUNTY LIBRARY
Government Documents
801 S.W. 10th Ave.
Portland 97205
(503) 248-5123

OREGON STATE LIBRARY
State Library Building
Salem 97310
(503) 378-4277

PENNSYLVANIA

NORTHAMPTON COMMUNITY COLLEGE
Learning Resources Center
3835 Green Pond Road
Bethlehem 18017
(610) 861-5360

ERIE COUNTY LIBRARY
160 E. Front St.
Erie 16507
(814) 451-6927

DAUPHIN COUNTY LIBRARY SYSTEM
Central Library
101 Walnut St.
Harrisburg 17101
(717) 234-4976

LANCASTER COUNTY PUBLIC LIBRARY
125 N. Duke St.
Lancaster 17602
(717) 394-2651

*FREE LIBRARY OF PHILADELPHIA
Regional Foundation Center
Logan Square
Philadelphia 19103
(215) 686-5423

*CARNEGIE LIBRARY OF PITTSBURGH
Foundation Collection
4400 Forbes Ave.
Pittsburgh 15213-4080
(412) 622-1917

POCONO NORTHEAST DEVELOPMENT FUND
James Pettinger Memorial Library
1151 Oak St.
Pittston 18640-3795
(570) 655-5581

READING PUBLIC LIBRARY
100 S. Fifth St.
Reading 19475
(610) 655-6355

MARTIN LIBRARY
159 Market St.
York 17401
(717) 846-5300

RHODE ISLAND

PROVIDENCE PUBLIC LIBRARY
225 Washington St.
Providence 02906
(401) 455-8088

SOUTH CAROLINA

ANDERSON COUNTY LIBRARY
202 E. Greenville St.
Anderson 29621
(864) 260-4500

*CHARLESTON COUNTY LIBRARY
68 Calhoun St.
Charleston 29401
(843) 805-6950

*SOUTH CAROLINA STATE LIBRARY
1500 Senate St.
Columbia 29211-1469
(803) 734-8666

COMMUNITY FOUNDATION OF GREATER
   GREENVILLE
27 Cleveland St., Suite 101
P.O. Box 6909
Greenville 29606
(864) 233-5925

SOUTH DAKOTA

*SOUTH DAKOTA STATE LIBRARY
800 Governors Drive
Pierre 57501-5070
(605) 773-3131
(800) 592-1841 (SD residents)

NONPROFIT MANAGEMENT INSTITUTE
132 S. Dakota Road
Sioux Falls 57102
(605) 367-5380

SIOUXLAND LIBRARIES
201 N. Main Ave.
Sioux Falls 57104
(605) 367-7081

TENNESSEE

*KNOX COUNTY PUBLIC LIBRARY
500 W. Church Ave.
Knoxville 37902
(423) 544-5750

*MEMPHIS & SHELBY COUNTY PUBLIC
   LIBRARY
1850 Peabody Ave.
Memphis 38104
(901) 725-8877

*NASHVILLE PUBLIC LIBRARY
Business Information Division
225 Polk Ave.
Nashville 37203
(615) 862-5842

TEXAS

NONPROFIT RESOURCE CENTER
Funding Information Library
500 N. Chestnut, Suite 1511
Abilene 79604
(915) 677-8166

*AMARILLO AREA FOUNDATION
700 First National Place
801 S. Fillmore
Amarillo 79101
(806) 376-4521

*HOGG FOUNDATION FOR MENTAL HEALTH
3001 Lake Austin Blvd.
Austin 78703
(512) 471-5041

*BEAUMONT PUBLIC LIBRARY
801 Pearl St.
Beaumont 77704-3827
(409) 838-6606

CORPUS CHRISTI PUBLIC LIBRARY
Funding Information Center
805 Comanche Street
Corpus Christi 78401
(361) 880-7000

*DALLAS PUBLIC LIBRARY
Urban Information
1515 Young St.
Dallas 75201
(214) 670-1487

SOUTHWEST BORDER NONPROFIT
  RESOURCE CENTER
1201 W. University Drive
Edinburgh 78539
(956) 316-2610

CENTER FOR VOLUNTEERISM & NONPROFIT
  MANAGEMENT
1918 Texas Ave.
El Paso 79901
(915) 532-5377

*FUNDING INFORMATION CENTER OF
  FORT WORTH
329 S. Henderson
Fort Worth 76104
(817) 334-0228

HOUSTON PUBLIC LIBRARY
Bibliographic Information Center
500 McKinney
Houston 77002
(713) 236-1313

NONPROFIT MANAGEMENT AND VOLUNTEER
  CENTER
Laredo Public Library
1120 E. Calton Road
Laredo 78041
(956) 795-2400

LONGVIEW PUBLIC LIBRARY
222 W. Cotton St.
Longview 75601
(903) 237-1352

LUBBOCK AREA FOUNDATION INC.
1655 Main St., Suite 209
Lubbock 79401
(806) 762-8061

*NONPROFIT RESOURCE CENTER OF TEXAS
111 Soledad, Suite 200
San Antonio 78205
(210) 227-4333

WACO-McLENNAN COUNTY LIBRARY
1717 Austin Ave.
Waco 76701
(254) 750-5975

NORTH TEXAS CENTER FOR NONPROFIT
  MANAGEMENT
624 Indiana, Suite 307
Wichita Falls 76301
(940) 322-496

UTAH

*SALT LAKE CITY PUBLIC LIBRARY
209 East 500 South
Salt Lake City 84111
(801) 524-8200

VERMONT

*VERMONT DEPT. OF LIBRARIES
Reference & Law Information Services
109 State St.
Montpelier 05609
(802) 828-3268

VIRGINIA

HAMPTON PUBLIC LIBRARY
4207 Victoria Blvd.
Hampton 23669
(757) 727-1312

*RICHMOND PUBLIC LIBRARY
Business, Science & Technology
101 E. Franklin St.
Richmond 23219
(804) 780-8223

*ROANOKE CITY PUBLIC LIBRARY SYSTEM
706 S. Jefferson St.
Roanoke 24016
(540) 853-2477

WASHINGTON

MID-COLUMBIA LIBRARY
405 S. Dayton
Kennewick 99336
(509) 586-3156

*SEATTLE PUBLIC LIBRARY
Science, Social Science
1000 Fourth Ave.
Seattle 98104
(206) 386-4620

*SPOKANE PUBLIC LIBRARY
Funding Information Center
811 W. Main Ave.
Spokane 99201
(509) 444-5336

UNITED WAY OF PIERCE COUNTY
Center for Nonprofit Development
1501 Pacific Ave., Suite 400
P.O. Box 2215
Tacoma 98401
(206) 272-4263

GREATER WENATCHEE COMMUNITY
  FOUNDATION AT THE WENATCHEE
  PUBLIC LIBRARY
310 Douglas St.
Wenatchee 98807
(509) 662-5021

WEST VIRGINIA

*KANAWHA COUNTY PUBLIC LIBRARY
123 Capitol St.
Charleston 25301
(304) 343-4646

WISCONSIN

*UNIVERSITY OF WISCONSIN-MADISON
Memorial Library
728 State St.
Madison 53706
(608) 262-3242

*MARQUETTE UNIVERSITY MEMORIAL
  LIBRARY
Funding Information Center
1415 W. Wisconsin Ave.
Milwaukee 53201-3141
(414) 288-1515

UNIVERSITY OF WISCONSIN-STEVENS
  POINT LIBRARY
Foundation Collection
900 Reserve St.
Stevens Point 54481-3897
(715) 346-4204

WYOMING

*NATRONA COUNTY PUBLIC LIBRARY
307 E. Second St.
Casper 82601-2598
(307) 237-4935

*LARAMIE COUNTY COMMUNITY COLLEGE
Instructional Resource Center
1400 E. College Drive
Cheyenne 82007-3299
(307) 778-1206

*CAMPBELL COUNTY PUBLIC LIBRARY
2101 4-J Road
Gillette 82718
(307) 687-0115

TETON COUNTY LIBRARY
125 Virginia Lane
Jackson 83001
(307) 733-2164

ROCK SPRINGS LIBRARY
400 C St.
Rock Springs 82901
(307) 362-6667

PUERTO RICO

UNIVERSIDAD DEL SAGRADO CORAZON
M.M.T. Guevara Library
Santurce 00914
(809) 728-1515 x 4357

➤ **The Council on Foundations.** This nonprofit membership organization was established in 1949 to promote "responsible and effective philanthropy." Members of the council include more than 1,200 different foundations, corporate giving programs and international grantmakers. Several resources are available from The Council on Foundations to help potential grantseekers. *Foundation News* magazine reports on current trends and activities in the private sector, while *Council Column* is a newsletter providing up-to-date information on foundation news.

For further information about the council, its members or publications, contact The Council on Foundations, 1828 L St. N.W., Suite 300, Washington, DC 20036; (202) 466-6512. The council's Web address is **http://www.cof.org**.

➤ **Other organizations**. There are also a number of other nonprofit organizations that can provide you with technical assistance and training to improve your grantwriting skills. Two of the most prominent organizations are The Grantsmanship Center and the Support Centers of America.

The Grantsmanship Center trains nonprofit executives by offering a range of resources, workshops and technical assistance services. It also maintains a database of current grant funding opportunities and offers online access to many of its publications and resources.

For further information, contact The Grantsmanship Center, 1125 W. Sixth St., Fifth Floor, Box 17220, Los Angeles, CA 90017; (213) 482–9860. Information is available online at **http://www.tgci.com.**

The Support Centers of America operates 12 regional centers that offer management training, consulting, technical assistance and support services to nonprofit leaders. You should contact one of the regional centers to find out about current training opportunities, workshops and similar special events.

Additional information, including contact information for regional centers, is available from Support Centers of America, 706 Mission St., Fifth Floor, San Francisco, CA 94103–9000; (415) 541–9000. The Web address is **http://www.supportcenter.org/sf/.**

➢ **Online Resources.** With the explosion in recent years of the Internet and online resources, grantseekers who have the time and the expertise to "surf the Web" can find a wealth of information on private giving. As mentioned above, The Foundation Center and The Council on Foundations both have extensive Web sites that are great places to begin a search for private funding information. In addition, almost every private grantmaker – from the largest corporate giving program to a small community foundation – maintains a Web site where you can find additional information about giving priorities, grantmaking guidelines and current funding opportunities.

Sources of Information on Federal Grants

➢ *Federal Register.* The *Federal Register* is the official government publication containing all final and proposed regulations, guidelines, announcements and notices of funding availability issued by federal agencies. Published daily, except for weekends and federal holidays, the *Federal Register* is an important resource for individuals seeking grants or contract support from the federal government. The annual subscription price for a print version of the *Federal Register* is $555. A microfiche version is available for $220. To order, call the Government Printing Office, (202) 512–1800. Free online access to the *Federal Register* is available at **http://www.access.gpo.gov/nara/index.html.**

➢ *Commerce Business Daily.* This publication, also issued on a daily basis, is a synopsis of federal proposed procurements, sales and contract awards. The *Commerce Business Daily* lists requests for proposals (RFPs) as well as contract awards for all federal agencies. The listings in this publication are strictly requests for equipment purchases, service contracts and research projects. You will not find grant funding opportunities listed in the *Commerce Business Daily.* The subscription price is $324 per year for first class mailing or $275 per year for second class mailing. Orders may be placed by contacting the Government Printing Office, (202) 512–1800.

➢ *Catalog of Federal Domestic Assistance (CFDA).* This two-volume guide is designed to help individuals identify the types of federal funding that is available. Each domestic program is listed individually by administering agency, with general information on program purpose, eligibility requirements and the types of assistance provided. The book is published each June and is updated in December. The *CFDA* is a good place to start when looking for grants, but you should use this guide as a reference. Because it is only updated twice a year, it does not provide you with information about which programs are currently accepting applications. The cost is $60. The catalog may be viewed online at **http://www.gsa.gov/fdac/default.htm**. For information, contact the General Services Administration, (202) 708–5126.

In addition to these resources, nearly every federal agency and organization, from the Department of Housing and Urban Development to the National Endowment for the Arts, has a Web site where you can find information about its programs, funding opportunities and current initiatives. In addition, the U.S. House of Representatives and Senate Web pages can help you keep track of what is going on in Congress, information that can be invaluable in predicting federal giving trends.

If you want to find a specific federal agency or department and do not know where to start, try accessing one of these sites:

➢ **The White House (http://www.whitehouse.gov/WH/EOP/html/ 3_parts.htm/).** This site will link you to all of the departments and agencies of the President's Cabinet, as well as independent federal agencies.

➢ **The U.S. Senate (http://www.senate.gov).** From here you can link to the home pages of Senate committees, as well as member offices.

➢ **The U.S. House of Representatives (http://www.house.gov).** Like the Senate Web site, this site offers descriptions about current events in the House, along with information about individual House members.

Index

K-L

Letter of support, 12
Lighthouse Project, 42

M

Management concerns, 54
Management plan, 41
Match, 13
Memorandum of understanding, 12
Medicare, 37
Minnesota Common Grant Application Form, 57, 59, 60, 61, 62
Minnesota Council on Foundations, 57

N

Narrative, 14
National Science Foundation, 58
Needs assessment, 10
Newman's Own Inc., 20
Notice of funding availability (NOFA), 38
Notice of intent to apply, 16

O

Objectives, 11
Online resources, 79
Organizational history, 11

P

Partnership, 11
Plan of operation, 11
Politically oriented organizations, 4
Poverty rate, 37
Preliminary proposal, 11
Priorities, 38, 53
Private foundation, 17
Private sector grants, 79
Problem statement, 10

Progress reports, 54
Project description, 11
Project design, 41
Project management, 54
Proposal reviewer, 40
Public charities, 17

Q

Qualified organizations, 39

R

Religion–oriented organizations, 4
Request for proposals (RFP), 18

S

Standard federal forms, 41, 57
Standard Form 424, 41, 57, 63, 64
Standard Form 424A, 41, 57, 65, 66, 67, 68
Standard Form 424B, 41, 57, 69, 70
Standard Form 424C, 41, 57, 71, 72
Standard Form 424D, 41, 57, 73, 74
Standard Form LLL, 41, 57, 75, 76
Subgrants, 37, 39
Support Centers of America, 92, 93

T

Technical assistance, 40
Temporary Assistance for Needy Families, 37

U

U.S. Government Printing Office, 40, 93
U.S. House of Representatives Web page, 94
U.S. Senate Web page, 94

V-W

White House Web page, 94
World Wide Web, 39